So you really want to learn

LATIN
PREP

BOOK 1

So you really want to learn

LATIN PREP

BOOK 1

Theo Zinn M.A. (Oxon.)

Series Editor: Nicholas Oulton M.A. (Oxon.)

GALORE PARK

Published by Galore Park Publishing Ltd.,
PO Box 96, Cranbrook TN17 4WS
www.galorepark.co.uk

Typography and layout by Typetechnique, London W1
Cover design by GKA Design, London WC2
Printed by Ashford Colour Press

ISBN 1 902984 15 3

First published 2003

Also available:
Teacher's resource book   1902984161

Acknowledgements

I should like to express my very special thanks to Nicholas Oulton for his courteous, shrewd and ruthless editing of this work; if it fulfils its aim, as I hope it does, this is chiefly due to him.

I thank also Peter Brown of Trinity College, Oxford who has constantly responded with such kindness and scholarliness to a veritable bombardment of telephone calls extending over many weeks.

And I thank Peter and Jackie Fennymore for their continual support, which contributed greatly to my completing this book.

Many thanks too to Rupert Fennymore whose outstanding IT skills averted many a crisis.

I need hardly say that all mistakes and infelicities are entirely my own work.

Author's preface

The first aim of this book is to introduce beginners to the 1st year Latin CE syllabus. I have adhered pretty faithfully to the vocabulary and usages required by this syllabus and that is partly my excuse for the rather unconventional style of some of my stories. In this context I must beg tolerance from my stricter readers for not being able to use the alarming verb *inquam* - not in the syllabus! - when direct speech is involved, as it so frequently has to be. Instead, I have permitted myself to use a host of other verbs such as *dīcō, clāmo, rogō, respondeō* etc. and have found, to my surprise and relief, that at least some of these verbs are used over and over again by Ovid to present direct speech. So I take refuge in claiming that my little stories, though not cast in any particular metre, are essentially poetic and are therefore entitled to poetic licence (it's a good try anyway!)

TLZ

Contents

Chapter 3

Chapter 4

Chapter 5

Chapter 6

Chapter 7

Chapter 8

Chapter 9

Chapter 10

Vocabularies

Introduction

Why Latin?

You have probably heard people say that Latin is useful because it helps us with our English. The reason for this is that around half the words you meet in English were used in some form or other by the Romans. The Romans, as I'm sure you know, ruled an empire which spread over much of Europe (as well as Asia Minor and North Africa). Their language, Latin, was spoken throughout this large empire but, over the decades and centuries, it changed. In Italy it gradually evolved into Italian; in Spain it became Spanish; and in Gaul (i.e. France) it became French. And so, when William the Conqueror conquered England in 1066, he brought with him his language (i.e. Norman-French). And it is from this language, Norman-French, that much of our own English language is derived. For example the word "irate" meaning "angry" comes from the Latin word *īra* = anger. The word "spectator" meaning "someone who watches" comes from the Latin word *spectō* = "I watch". The more Latin words you learn, the more you will realise how much of our English language is in fact taken directly (or indirectly) from Julius Caesar and his merry men. And all thanks to the Battle of Hastings!

For this reason alone one should not be on the defensive in claiming that it is a good idea to learn Latin. But there is another reason too; Latin is a most wonderful and beautiful language, and although so much Latin literature has been lost or destroyed, the fragment that remains bears comparison with any other literature in existence.

Latin is difficult, certainly, but not absurdly so. I have tried in this book to supply you with a sound basis for mastering Latin and this process will continue in Books 2 and 3 of this course. You may think that in this book I sometimes approach certain features of Latin a little disrespectfully. I would like to think rather that my approach embodies the kind of familiary and jocularity which we often display with someone we love. Certainly, I love the Latin language as a language, with all its rules and irregularities: I love everything about it. Indeed I would not hesitate to say that, even if there were no Latin *literature* at all, the language itself is one of the greatest monuments of human creativity and fully justifies the learning of it.

You may have heard people talking airily about Latin being a dead language. We have already pointed out that it is in fact very much alive in the languages derived or partially derived from it. Probably people mean that Latin itself is now simply a written language and is no longer spoken (except on some formal occasions in universities and the like). But this approach is misleading since, in the days when Latin *was* spoken, books were by our standards extremely rare and books were regularly read aloud. Certainly Latin falls beautifully upon the ear and one should

Read the following passage and answer the questions that follow.

The dangers of Danegeld?

1　*agricolae et nautae pugnant: agricolae hastīs et nautae*
sagittīs pugnant. īnsulae rēgīna agricolīs et nautīs
pecūniam dat: <u>nōn iam</u> pugnant. Sulpicia fēmina est:
Cassia puella est. agricolās et nautās spectant. <u>mox</u>
5　*Sulpicia et Cassia pugnant. <u>diū</u> pugnant et <u>tandem</u> "ubi*
est pecūnia?" clāmat Sulpicia. "rēgīna agricolīs et nautīs
pecūniam dat. etiam fēminārum rēgīna et puellārum est.
fēminae <u>tamen</u> et puellae pecūniam rēgīna nōn dat."
"rēgīna, fēminās et puellās nōn amās!" clāmat Cassia.
10　*"nōs <u>igitur</u> rēgīnam nōn amāmus!"*

pecūnia, -ae, f. = money
nōn iam = no longer
mox = soon
diū = for a long time
tandem = at last
tamen = however
igitur = therefore

1.　Translate the passage into beautiful English prose.

2.　Give one example from the passage of the following:

(a) a noun in the nominative singular
(b) a noun in the nominative plural
(c) a noun in the accusative singular
(d) a noun in the accusative plural
(e) a noun in the genitive singular

(f) a noun in the genitive plural
(g) a noun in the dative singular
(h) a noun in the dative plural
(i) a noun in the ablative plural
(j) a noun in the vocative singular

Fi:
1.
2.
3.
4.
5.
6.
7.
8.
9.
10

take every opportunity to read it aloud. It is utterly a language that should be read aloud, because only in so doing and in doing it well, can you fully appreciate the beauty of which I have spoken. I suggest then that, from the start, you read lots of Latin, even simple words, aloud; and try to relish them. In the course of this book I have occasionally reminded you of this.

Pronunciation

To the Roman ear there was an immensely important difference between a long and a short vowel. To ignore the **quantity** (i.e. the length) of a vowel is rather the same as to play the piano from piano music without worrying too much about "silly little things" such as whether a note is black or white or whether it has a tail or tails or is tail-less (I hope you like this word). Incidentally, a lot more is known about the pronunciation of Latin than you may think.

Short vowels

Very nearly all vowels in this book are assumed to be short unless marked as long (see below). Occasionally we have marked a vowel as being short, but only if there is a definite and inescapable tendency to pronounce it incorrectly. Where vowels are marked short, we do this with a little sign called a breve (e.g. *ă, ĕ, ĭ, ŏ, ŭ*).

> A short *ă* is pronounced something like "u" in "hut". E.g. *ad* (= to).
> A short *ĕ* is pronounced something like "e" in "neck". E.g. *sed* (= but).
> A short *ĭ* is pronounced something like "i" in "hit". E.g. *cibus* (= food).
> A short *ŏ* is pronounced something like "o" in "lot". E.g. *novem* (= nine).
> A short *ŭ* is pronounced something like "oo" in "hood". E.g. *cum* (= with).

Long vowels

All vowels that are long are marked with a sign called a macron (e.g. *ā, ē, ī, ō, ū*).

> A long *ā* is pronounced something like "ar" in "far". E.g. *ā* (= from).
> A long *ē* is pronounced something like "ai" in "bait". E.g. *mē* (= me).
> A long *ī* is pronounced something like "ee" in "feet". E.g. *hīc* (= here).
> A long *ō* is pronounced something like "oa" in "boar". E.g. *nōs* (= we).
> A long *ū* is pronounced something like "oo" in pool; (*never* the "yu" noise in "fume".) E.g. *tū* (= you).

Long "*ē*"s and long "*ō*"s are a little more complicated than this, really, but if you follow these instructions you might only be a semi-tone wrong, if that! And in some words the Romans could not make up their minds about the letter "*i*". Thus in the words *ubi* = "when" and *ibi* = "there", the final "*i*" is sometimes treated as short, sometimes as long. Having told you this, we feel no qualms about leaving it unmarked.

A vowel is *always* long before -*ns* and -*nf*, even *between* words.

> Eg. *īnsula* (= island).
> Eg. *īn sacrō locō* (= in a sacred place).

Always give vowels their full (and correct) value when pronouncing words. For example *regere* (= to rule) has three identical short "*e*" sounds: *re-ge-re*.

Diphthongs

When two vowels are pronounced as one syllable, they create a diphthong.

> *AE* is pronounced something like "i" in "tie". E.g. *laetus* (= happy).
> *AU* is pronounced something like "ow" in "cow". E.g. *nauta* (= sailor).
> *EI* is pronounced something like "ay" in "day". E.g. *deinde* (= then).
> *OE* is pronounced something like "oy" in "boy". E.g. *Poenus* (= Carthaginian).

Beware, however, of the word *poēta* (= poet). In this word the 'oe' is not a diphthong; the 'o' and the 'e' are two separate vowels, giving the word three lovely syllables in all: *po-ē-ta*.

EU is a hard one; luckily, not many Latin words use this, though it does occur in Greek names (e.g. Theseus). Try to pronounce a short *e* (as in pet) and a short *u* (as in put) so close to each other that they produce a single sound. Try this with the word *heu*, which rather appropriately means "alas!" Do not make it sound like the name Hugh.

Consonants

Most consonants in Latin are pronounced as they are in English. However, look out for the following:

> *C* is always hard, as in "cat". E.g. *Caesar* begins with a hard "c" noise, <u>not</u> the soft "s" noise that we tend to use in English.
>
> *G* is always hard, as in "gun". E.g. *rēgīna* (= queen).
>
> Consonantal "*i*"; the letter "*i*" is generally a vowel, but it can also be used as the English letter "y" (in words such as "you"). Hence the Latin word *iam* (= now) is pronounced "yum". In the past it was written with a "*j*" (from the German "j" which is pronounced like our consonantal "y") and this led to its being pronounced like our letter "j" (as in "jam"). But this was wrong. (See page 80.)
>
> *R* is always rolled, using the tip of the tongue (if you are lucky enough to be able to do this). E.g. *portō* (= I carry). Note also that vowels before "r" are not automatically lengthened as they tend to be in English. Thus the first "o" in the Latin word *portō* is short, and should not be "stretched" as in our English word "porter".
>
> *S* is always as "s" in "silly", never the "z" noise in words such as "busy". E.g. *quis?* (= who?).
>
> *V* is always as the "w" in "water". E.g. *veniō* (= I come).
>
> *Y* exists only in names that come from Greek, and should be pronounced like a French "u". E.g. *Hymettus* (a mountain near Athens).

CH, PH, TH come from Greek and should not be pronounced as they are in English. They are pronounced as very hard Cs, Ps and Ts respectively (i.e. ignoring the "h"). E.g. *Charōn, Philippī* and *Thēseus*.

GN is pronounced NGN as in "hangnail". E.g. *magnus* (= big) is pronounced "mungnoos".

Finally, note that when you meet a double consonant in Latin, as in *puella* (= girl), or *terra* (= earth), we should linger on the two consonants and try to give each its full value.

The false quantity

As we have said, the length of a vowel is called its quantity. In the old days, if you got a quantity wrong, you had perpetrated a "false quantity", and were obliged to bow your head in shame and to consider yourself the lowest of the low. Nearly all textbooks and grammars use macrons to mark the long vowels for you, as we do in this book. But the Romans didn't use these macrons themselves; they just knew. And when you learn a word, you should ideally include mastering its quantities as part of your learning. This is best done by pronouncing each word to yourself aloud as you learn it. For example: *Rōmānus* (= Roman). Say its three syllables aloud slowly, *Rō-mā-nus*, making sure that you have two nice long vowels followed by one short one. Now this sort of thing is part of the fun of learning this beautiful language. Indeed false quantites could be most embarrassing. Pity the poor farmer who cried out to his wife "*mea uxor est mala sūs*" which means – I can hardly bring myself to translate it – "my wife is a bad pig." (Actually, I believe that pigs are very clean and pleasant animals). History does not record what followed upon his remark, though I am told that the lady was carrying a thick broom at the time. What he had *meant* to say was "*meā, uxor, ēst māla sūs*" which means "move, wife, the pig is eating the apples!" You just can't be too careful.

And now... into the deep end!

When you turn the page you are going to be thrown, fully-clothed, into the deep-end. But fear not, everything will very soon be explained. It is like one of those films which begin right in the middle of the story, with all sorts of people you don't know and all sorts of mysterious things happening, and then suddenly you are taken back to the beginning and you start to understand what it is all about. The opening scenes give you a feel for the whole thing, as a sort of "taster", before you settle down to work out who is who and what is what. So, here we go!

Chapter 1

Salvē!

Welcome! Assuming that you are normal (like me?), you will have skipped the Introduction, but I suggest that you go back to it now, particularly to the bit about pronunciation. You may also like to have a little peep at the vocabulary below. Then read aloud and see if you can make sense of the following:

Sulpicia fēmina est.

Aulus agricola est.

ego Sulpicia sum.
fēmina sum.

ego Aulus sum.
agricola sum.

ego Quīntus sum.
poēta sum.

"*Salvē, Sulpicia. ubi est Mārcus?*"
"*Mārcus hīc est. etiam Cassia hīc est. Cassia puella est.*"

"*quis est Quīntus?*"
"*Quīntus poēta est.*"

"*Cassia, ubi sunt Aulus et Sulpicia?*"
"*Aulus et Sulpicia hīc sunt.*"

Claudia et Cassia puellae sunt. Rōmānae puellae sunt.
"*salvē. nōs puellae sumus.*"

etiam Laelia puella Rōmāna est.
"*salvē. puella Rōmāna sum.*"

Gnaeus Rōmānus est. Sextus Rōmānus est.
Gnaeus et Sextus agricolae nōn sunt. nautae sunt.
"*salvē. nōs nautae sumus.*"

Vocabulary

salvē = greetings, hello	*sunt* = (they) are
agricola = farmer	*hīc* = here
fēmina = woman	*etiam* = also, even
puella = girl	*quis?* = who?
poēta = poet	*ubi?* = where?
nauta = sailor	*et* = and
Rōmānus = Roman	*ego* = I
sum = I am	*tū* = you (singular)
est = (he, she or it) is	*nōs* = we
sumus = we are	*vōs* = you (plural)
	nōn = not

A bit about endings...

You will have noticed (no doubt) that some of the Latin names above end in *-a* and others end in *-us*. The ones in *-a* refer to females (e.g. *Claudia*, *Sulpicia*, *Cassia* and *Laelia*), the ones in *-us* (*Aulus*, *Mārcus*, *Sextus*, *Gnaeus* and *Quīntus*) to males. In the same way a female Roman was *Rōmāna* and a male Roman was *Rōmānus*. This business of Latin words changing their endings is a vital part of the language, so we need to get used to it right from the start.

Mārcus Rōmānus est.

Sulpicia Rōmāna est.

Singular and plural

Nouns in Latin, just as in English, can be either singular or plural. In English we generally (but not always) make a noun plural by adding "s". In Latin it is rather more complicated than this, but if the noun ends in *-a* (e.g. *agricola* or *puella*), it changes to *-ae* in the plural.

Singular	**Plural**
puella = the girl	*puellae* = the girls
agricola = the farmer	*agricolae* = the farmers

Exercise 1.1

Using the nouns below, make them plural, as in the example.

E.g.   The girl = *puella*;   the girls = *puellae*.

1.   The island = *īnsula*
2.   The poet = *poēta*
3.   The sailor = *nauta*
4.   The arrow = *sagitta*
5.   The spear = *hasta*

To be or not to be?

We are now going to think about a few of the words used above, in particular *est* and *sunt*.
You probably guessed what these meant when you first saw them, and if you didn't, you could have done, because they are very similar to the French words *est* and *sont*. These words are part of the first Latin verb that we are going to learn, the verb "to be". Although this is an irregular verb, and no other verb goes like it, it occurs so often that we just can't do without it:

1st person singular	*sum*	=	I am
2nd person singular	*es*	=	you (singular) are
3rd person singular	*est*	=	he, she or it is
1st person plural	*sumus*	=	we are
2nd person plural	*estis*	=	you (plural) are
3rd person plural	*sunt*	=	they are

Notice, then, how similar this is to the French verb *être*, which means exactly the same thing (although French verbs, like English ones, are slightly feeble and need pronouns to help them along: *je, tu, il/elle* etc.). In Latin, such pronouns are used mainly for emphasis.

E.g.   *ego agricola sum, tū nauta es* = I am a farmer, *you* are a sailor.

A or the?

The word "the" is called the **definite article** and the word "a" is called the **indefinite article**. In Latin, however, there are no definite or indefinite articles; in other words there is no word in Latin for "a" or for "the". Thus, *puella* can mean "a girl" or "the girl". For example "*ubi est puella?*" means "where is *the* girl?" rather than "where is *a* girl?", only if it makes better sense that way. Often, either "a" or "the" could be right and you are allowed to decide (big of us, eh?). Similarly, in the plural we have a choice between "girls" and "*the* girls".

ubi est puella

Exercise 1.2

Translate into English, choosing (where appropriate) between "a" and "the":

1. *quis hīc est?*
2. *Aulus hīc est.*
3. *poēta et agricola hīc sunt.*
4. *Sulpicia et Laelia Rōmānae sunt.*
5. *Quīntus et Aulus hīc sunt.*
6. *ubi est fēmina Rōmāna?*
7. *puella Rōmāna et agricola Rōmānus hīc sunt.*
8. *ego sum Sulpicia, tū es Laelia.*
9. *nōs nautae sumus.*
10. *vōs agricolae estis.*

Note that in most of these sentences some part of the verb *sum* comes at the end. On the whole, the Romans liked ending their sentences with a verb. Notice also that Latin sentences start with a small letter, except when the first word is a name. You may have thought we were being lazy, but we weren't.

Pronouns

As we have seen, pronouns in Latin are used mainly for emphasis. But you need to know them, so here are the 1st and 2nd person pronouns again. We will leave the 3rd person ones (he, she, it and they) until much later.

	Singular	**Plural**
1st person	*ego* = I	*nōs* = we
2nd person	*tū* = you	*vōs* = you

Exercise 1.3

Translate into Latin, using pronouns for the words in italics, as in the example.

E.g.   *I* am a farmer = *ego agricola sum*.

1. *You* are a girl but *I* am a woman.
2. *We* are farmers, but* *you* are sailors.
3. *You* are Quintus.
4. *You* (plural) are girls.
5. *You* are Sulpicia, but *I* am Laelia.

N.B. *sed* = but

ego agricola sum

The Roman Empire

As you can see from the map below, the Romans carved out quite an empire for themselves. The area shaded in pink shows the extent of their empire in the year 117 AD.

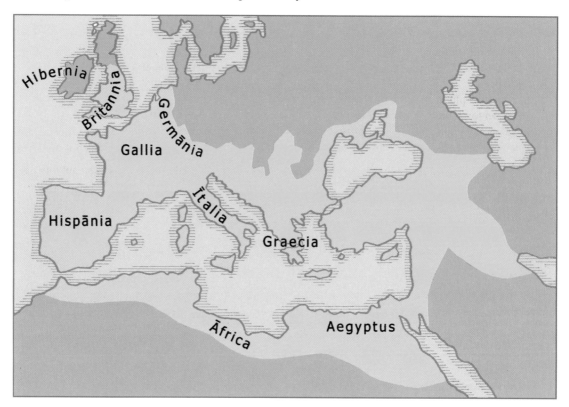

Exercise 1.4

Study the map above. Write down the Latin names for the following modern day countries:

1. Britain
2. France
3. Germany
4. Italy
5. Spain
6. Ireland

Exercise 1.5

Give English words that originate from the following Latin ones. You have met some of these Latin words already, but some of them you will have to look up in the vocabulary at the back (or you might even be able to guess their meanings by thinking of the English words that come from them).

E.g.   *īra* = anger; English word: irate.

1. *aqua*
2. *fēmina*
3. *poēta*
4. *agricola*
5. *nauta*
6. *patria*
7. *īnsula*
8. *ego*

Amō = I love: present tense

We have already met *sum*, which was an irregular (but very important) verb, but now we are going to see how regular verbs work. We will begin with *amō* = "I love". Here it is in full in the **present tense**; needless to say, you need to look carefully at the **ending** of each word:

1st person singular	*amō*	=	I love
2nd person singular	*amās*	=	you (singular) love
3rd person singular	*amat*	=	he, she or it loves
1st person plural	*amāmus*	=	we love
2nd person plural	*amātis*	=	you (plural) love
3rd person plural	*amant*	=	they love

Note how the **endings -ō, -s, -t, -mus, -tis, -nt** are added to the **stem** *amā-/ama-*. The observant among you will notice that the 1st person singular (*amō*) uses a slightly squashed stem (*am-*) but fear not, the missing "*a*" comes bouncing back in the 2nd person and is rarely absent again. Note also that in the third persons the final "*a*" of the stem is short.

Verbs like amō

The great thing about regular verbs is that they all go the same way! Thus verbs that go like *amō* all belong to a family of verbs called the 1st conjugation, adding the same endings and generally behaving in a nice, regular way. Here, to prove it, is the verb *cantō*:

1st person singular	*cantō*	=	I sing
2nd person singular	*cantās*	=	you (singular) sing
3rd person singular	*cantat*	=	he, she or it sings
1st person plural	*cantāmus*	=	we sing
2nd person plural	*cantātis*	=	you (plural) sing
3rd person plural	*cantant*	=	they sing

See how the endings are exactly the same as they were for *amō*? It is only the stem that is different.

Exercise 1.6

Copying the beautiful table above, write out in full the present tense of any *four* of the following 1st conjugation verbs (which all go like *amō*), including the meanings:

aedificō	=	I build		*habitō*	=	I inhabit, live, dwell
ambulō	=	I walk		*labōrō*	=	I work
clāmō	=	I shout		*laudō*	=	I praise
rogō	=	I ask, ask for		*necō*	=	I kill, murder
festīnō	=	I hurry		*vocō*	=	I call

Exercise 1.7

Re-arrange the following parts of these verbs in the correct order:

1. *aedificat, aedificō, aedificāmus, aedificās, aedificant, aedificātis.*
2. *ambulās, ambulat, ambulō, ambulātis, ambulant, ambulāmus.*
3. *habitant, habitāmus, habitās, habitō, habitat, habitātis.*
4. *festīnāmus, festīnō, festīnat, festīnās, festīnant, festīnātis.*
5. *clāmātis, clāmat, clāmās, clāmant, clāmō, clāmāmus.*

Translating the present tense

In English we have three ways of expressing a present tense. For example, using the verb "to work" we can say "I work", "I am working" and "I do work". Each has a slightly different sense. But in Latin, hooray, hooray, there is only one form for the present tense, in this case *labōrō*. I suggest you stop for a minute and think how lucky you are not to be a Roman trying to learn English. Just imagine how hard the next exercise would be.

Exercise 1.8

Translate into English, using all three forms of the English present tense, as in the example.

E.g.   *clāmant* = they shout; they are shouting; they do shout.

1.	*vocāmus*		6.	*clāmat*
2.	*habitātis*		7.	*labōrātis*
3.	*amant*		8.	*necant*
4.	*ambulās*		9.	*festīnās*
5.	*aedificō*		10.	*cantāmus*

Exercise 1.9

Translate into Latin, as in the examples. You may need the vocabulary below for some of these.

E.g.   We are shouting = *clāmāmus*.
E.g.   He does not shout = *nōn clāmat*.

1.	She hurries.		6.	The farmer is shouting.
2.	They are singing.		7.	I ask.
3.	You (singular) walk.		8.	They are killing.
4.	Aulus is not singing.		9.	We call.
5.	Sulpicia works.		10.	They do not hurry.

Vocabulary

In this course we are going to learn 200 Latin words, twenty per chapter. These words need to be learnt by heart, both from Latin into English (easy) and from English into Latin (a bit harder). The best way to cope with vocabulary-learning is to keep a neat vocabulary book with all the words you need and to think of a good way of remembering the words. Often there is an English word that will remind you of the Latin one. In addition to these vocabularies at the end of each chapter, there will be little lists of words throughout the book that you may need to help you with a particular exercise. Most of these words will find their way into one of the ten main vocabularies, but because we only have twenty per chapter, you may have to be patient before some of them appear. So here are your first twenty words.

Vocabulary 1

aedificō = I build
ambulō = I walk
amō = I love, like
cantō = I sing
clāmō = I shout
dō* = I give
ego = I
et = and
festīnō = I hurry
habitō = I inhabit, live, dwell

labōrō = I work
laudō = I praise
necō = I kill
nōs = we
pugnō = I fight
rogō = I ask, ask for
sum = I am
tū = you (singular)
vocō = I call
vōs = you (plural)

---

*Note that, except in the 2nd person singular, *dās*, the "*a*" of *dō* is short:

dō	I give
dās	you (sing.) give
dat	he, she, it gives
dămus	we give
dătis	you give
dant	they give

Here endeth the first chapter, and not a minute too soon.

Chapter 2

A bit more about nouns

We must now get to grips in a big way with **nouns**. First, how do we recognise a noun? We are usually taught that a noun is a person, place or thing, but it is even easier to say that if we come across a word and can say that it IS something (or if plural, that they ARE something), then we are dealing with a noun. So when we say, for example, "my grandmother IS kind" or "these books ARE heavy"or "joy IS a feeling", the words grandmother, books and joy must all be nouns.

If a noun can be seen, heard, smelt, tasted or, especially, touched, it is a concrete noun; if not, it is an abstract noun. Thus "grandmother" and "books" are concrete nouns, while "joy" and "history" are abstract nouns. Luckily this need not worry us unduly but it's nice to know, isn't it?

The other thing you need to know about nouns in Latin is that they can be one of three **genders**: masculine, feminine or neuter (m., f. or n.). If a noun is neither masculine nor feminine (poor thing) it is said to be neuter. We will learn why these genders are important later.

Exercise 2.1

Which of the following English words are nouns? Say which are concrete and which are abstract.

1. Farmer
2. Poet
3. Angry
4. Freedom
5. Free

6. Hippopotamus
7. Anxiety
8. Teacher
9. Teachers
10. Teaches

1st declension nouns

Nouns in Latin belong to groups or families called declensions. The first type of noun we are going to study belongs to the 1st declension, which consists of nouns that end in *-a* such as *fēmina* and *puella* and *Claudia*. The vast majority of these nouns are feminine and they decline* as follows:

	Singular	Plural
Nominative	*puella*	*puellae*
Vocative	*puella*	*puellae*
Accusative	*puellam*	*puellās*
Genitive	*puellae*	*puellārum*
Dative	*puellae*	*puellīs*
Ablative	*puellā*	*puellīs*

*A puzzling use of the word. Decline means "to become less" or "to refuse". As far as I can see, it means something like "to go off the rails" here, which is rather a nice idea (I hope you agree).

You will learn soon why we have put some of the endings in green and some in red. Until such time, just note that very few 1st declension nouns are masculine, and the masculine ones you need to know are all types of people who, in the ancient world at least, were generally *men*: thus *poēta* (a poet) is masculine and so are *agricola* (a farmer) and *nauta* (a sailor). (By the way, you will be glad to hear that there is a special word for "poetess", though I don't know of any for "farmeress" or "sailoress".) And do be sure to note that the final "a" of *puellā* in the ablative singular is long, and sounds quite different from the short *a* in the nominative and vocative singular.

So, isn't this beautiful! – but whatever does it all mean?

Stems and endings

We have already learnt how to make some Latin nouns plural by changing *-a* to *-ae* at the end of the word. But now look what has happened; look at all these different forms of the word *puella*. What on earth is it all about? Well then, have a good look. Notice how the stem *puell-* is there all the way through and then on to *puell-* are added all sorts of different endings (shown in bold). But what do these endings do? They create cases. And what are cases (I hear you say)? Cases are the six words with strange names on the extreme left of the box above (and you won't be surprised to learn that these words all come from Latin). Learning how to use these cases is one of the great joys of learning Latin and you will soon be in the thick of it!

Exercise 2.2

Write out the following nouns in full, copying *puella* above. Set it all out exactly as *puella* is set out, with the cases on the left and the singular and plural next to each other in two neat columns (this is the hardest part, at least it always was for me). Whenever you write out (decline) a noun in full, that is how you should do it.

1. *fēmina* = woman
2. *agricola* = farmer
3. *hasta* = spear

The nominative case

As we have said, there are six cases. We will begin at the beginning (how original!). The **nominative case** is the one we use when we want to refer to a noun. Thus when someone asks "What is the Latin for girl?" the answer is *puella* (i.e. the word for a girl in the nominative case). But there is much more to the nominative than that, so hang on to your hats and learn these two vital facts by heart:

- The nominative case is used to express the subject of the verb.
- The subject of the verb is the person (or thing) who is doing the verb.

For example, in the sentence "the farmer is stroking the dog," it is the farmer who is doing the stroking; he is therefore the subject. In the sentence "the women are Roman," it is the women who are being Roman; they are therefore the subject. Thus the Latin for farmer (in the first sentence) and women (in the second one) would go into the nominative case. What's more, in some sentences there could be more than one subject. For example, in the sentence "Aulus and Marcus are Romans", Aulus and Marcus are both subjects (as they are both busily being Romans) and they would both go into the nominative case, joined together with the word *et* (= and). What joy!

Exercise 2.3

Copy the following exercises and underline the subject or subjects of the sentence, as in the example.

E.g.   <u>Quintus</u> is a poet.

1.   The dog is barking.
2.   The girls are singing.
3.   Sulpicia and Aulus are singing.
4.   Laelia is a woman.
5.   Aulus is a farmer.

Exercise 2.4

Give the Latin for the following nouns when these are the **subject** of the sentence:

1.   The poet
2.   A girl
3.   The girls
4.   Sulpicia and Cassia
5.   Farmers

Exercise 2.5

Read the following passage aloud and then answer the questions that follow.

Island life

1　*Cassia puella est; Aulus agricola est. Cassia cantat et Aulus clāmat. "cūr clāmās?" Cassia rogat. Sulpicia fēmina est; Quīntus poēta est. Sulpicia et Quīntus cantant. "cūr cantātis?" Claudia et Aulus rogant. "ubi*

5　*sumus?" rogat Laelia. "hīc terra est, hīc undae sunt; īnsula est," clāmat Lūcius.*

Gnaeus et Sextus nautae sunt. Lūcius et Mārcus agricolae sunt. nautae et agricolae pugnant. puellae et fēminae nōn pugnant. rēgina vocat et ancillae festīnant.

10　*"cūr pugnant agricolae et nautae?" rēgina rogat. "nautae sunt; agricolae sunt," ancillae clāmant. "nautae et agricolae semper pugnant." īnsula est!*

cūr? = why?

unda, f. = wave

rēgina, f. = queen
ancilla, f. = maid-servant

semper = always

1.　Translate the passage into English.

2.　Answer the following questions:
　　(a)　*Quīntus* (line 3): in which case is this noun?
　　(b)　*cantant* (line 4): why is this verb plural?
　　(c)　In line 8, what are the sailors and farmers doing?
　　(d)　In line 9, what do the maid-servants do when the queen calls?
　　(e)　Lines 10-12: why, according to the maid-servants, are the sailors and farmers fighting?

The vocative case

Our next case is the **vocative case** which is used if you are calling or addressing someone.
In the sentence "Aulus, come here!", Aulus is being called and therefore goes into the vocative case.
In the 1st declension, the ending for the vocative case is the same as that for the nominative case
(but things will become more exciting when we meet the 2nd declension).

Exercise 2.6

Copy the following sentences and underline the noun or nouns that would go into the vocative case, as in the example below. Remember there may be more than one in each sentence.

E.g.   <u>Sulpicia</u>, come here please.

1.   Cassia, where are you?
2.   Laelia, why are you crying?
3.   Laelia and Marcus, why are you shouting?

4.   Marcus is singing, Sulpicia.
5.   Hello, girls!

Exercise 2.7

Give the Latin for the underlined words only:

1.   <u>Sulpicia</u>, why are you sad?
2.   <u>Girls</u>, where are your friends?
3.   Marcus and Laelia are singing, <u>Cassia</u>.

4.   <u>Laelia and Cassia</u>, please sit down!
5.   <u>Farmers</u>, where are the horses?

Subjects and objects

We now come to a hugely important lesson, namely how to use the accusative case. Getting this wrong can lead to tears in a big way, so beware.

- The accusative case is used to express the object of the verb.

- The object is the person or thing which is at the receiving end of the verb.

E.g.   in the sentence "The man is stroking the dog", the dog is the one getting stroked and is therefore the object of the verb and goes into the accusative.

E.g.   in the sentence "The frog is kissing the princess", the princess is the one getting kissed (yuk) so she is the object of the verb and goes into the accusative.

You can see how important it is to get this right – particularly if you are a princess (or a frog for that matter)!

Exercise 2.8

In the following sentences, say which nouns are subjects (S) and which are objects (O), as in the example. You might like also to mark the verbs (V). If you are feeling very artistic, use **GREEN** for the subjects and the verbs and **RED** for the objects. The reason for this will become apparent later, so do stick to green and red.

	S	V	O
E.g.	The cat	eats	the mouse.

1. The woman loves the daughter.
2. The farmer watches the girls.
3. The girl calls the farmer.
4. The poet loves the goddess.
5. The farmer kills the maid-servant.

Exercise 2.9

Into what case would we put the nouns in each of the above sentences?

E.g. in sentence no. 1, "the woman", being the subject, goes into the nominative case and "the daughter", being the object, goes into the accusative.

Transitive and intransitive

While we are on this we should learn to distinguish between transitive and intransitive verbs. Transitive verbs are generally followed by (or *may* be followed by) an object; intransitive verbs are not.

E.g. *necō* (= I murder) is transitive (when murdering, one generally murders *someone*), while *ambulō* (= I walk) is intransitive (one cannot *walk* someone or something).

Exercise 2.10

Say whether the following Latin verbs are transitive or intransitive:

1. *amō*
2. *festīnō*
3. *aedificō*
4. *labōrō*
5. *laudō*

Note that *habitō* is either intransitive (meaning "I dwell") or transitive (meaning "I inhabit").

It is therefore somewhat misleading to say that *habitō* = I live (which is what most people do say!)

Exercise 2.11

Copy the following sentences, writing S over the subject, V over the verb and O over the object. Then translate into English.

        S.   O.   V.
E.g. *Cassia deam   amat* = Cassia loves the goddess.

1. *puella nautam vocat.*
2. *agricola patriam amat.*
3. *fēmina deam laudat.*
4. *nauta aquam nōn amat.*
5. *nauta īnsulam habitat.*
6. *puella ancillās vocat.*

Exercise 2.12

Copy the following sentences, writing S over the subject, V over the verb and O over the object. Then put the underlined words into LATIN, as in the example. The verbs have been done for you, and these words go at the end of the sentence. Note that all Latin names ending in -*a* belong to the first declension and thus go like *puella*.

	S	V	O		S	O	V
E.g.	Cassia	loves	the goddess	=	*Cassia*	*deam*	*amat.*
1.	Laelia	calls	the girl	=	___	___	*vocat*
2.	Sulpicia	does not like	poets	=	___	___	*nōn amat*
3.	The girls	watch	the maid-servants	=	___	___	*spectant*
4.	Sulpicia	praises	the farmer	=	___	___	*laudat*
5.	The sailors	kill	the farmer	=	___	___	*necant*

Exercise 2.13

Copy the following sentences, writing S over the subject, V over the verb and O over the object. Then translate into Latin, remembering to put the verb at the end of the sentence.

        S   V   O   S   O   V
E.g. Claudia loves   the land   =   *Claudia terram amat.*

1. The woman loves the daughter.
2. Laelia loves the goddess.
3. The farmer murders a maid-servant.
4. Sulpicia calls the sailor.
5. The sailor loves islands.
6. The goddess watches the girls.
7. The poet does not praise the inhabitants.
8. The girl calls the poets.

Traffic-lights: beware!

There is something you should note before we go much further. In English, we know *who* is doing something, and to *whom* they are doing it, by the order of the words. For example when we say that Marcus is murdering Aulus, we know that Marcus is the one doing the murdering because he is mentioned first. But in Latin it is not the word order but the *ending* on the noun that tells us who is doing something:

E.g.   *puella agricolam amat*; and
       agricolam puella amat

both mean the same thing: the girl loves the farmer.

We know the girl is the subject because *puella* is in the nominative case. We know the farmer is the object because *agricolam* is in the accusative case. It doesn't matter which way round the sentence is written.

Now of course you won't always have these beautiful colours there to help you; but you will always have the **endings**. So always, always, always look at the ending of a Latin word. The ending of a noun tells us which case it is in, and the ending of a verb tells us who is doing the verb. Think of a traffic-light; **green for go**, **red for stop**. Always **go** for the verb and its subject first, always **stop** before getting to an object (until you have found the subject and verb). Get this right and you will have no trouble in Latin. Get it wrong and you will be forever muddling your subjects with your objects, a terrible crime.

Exercise 2.14

Copy the following sentences. Mark **S** for subject, **V** for verb and **O** for object and then translate them into English. Remember, it is the case of the noun, not the word order, that tells us who or what is the subject and who or what is the object.

1.   *agricolae īnsulam habitant.*
2.   *deam puella amat.*
3.   *ancillae poētam vocant.*
4.   *fīliam fēmina spectat*
5.   *puellae rēgīnam laudant.*
6.   *rēgīnam puellae laudant.*

Cavē (beware, again!)

Another pitfall to look out for is when the subject of a sentence is hidden inside the verb.

E.g.   *fābulam nārrat* = he/she is telling a story.

It is often very tempting to take the first word in a sentence first and assume that it is the subject, but this can lead to terrible trouble. In our example above, the first word (*fābulam*) is in the accusative case, and so cannot possibly be the subject. But where *is* the subject? The subject is the pronoun (he or she) which is tucked away inside the verb. If the subject is tucked away inside the verb, it is helpful to mark it as follows:

O   V+S
puellam   amat = he/she loves the girl.

It is because a verb must have a subject, and because in Latin the two can be squeezed into one word, that we have been using green for both the subject and the verb. Clever, don't you think? But beware! If there is a noun in the nominative case lurking around in the Latin sentence, it becomes extremely stroppy. In fact it dismisses the poor old pronoun that seemed so safe, wrapped up in the verb, and takes over from it altogether.

E.g.   *amat* = he/she loves; but
       agricola amat = the farmer loves.
E.g.   *cantant* = they sing; but
       puellae cantant = the girls sing.

Only if there is no noun in the nominative to "govern" the verb (govern, if you please!) can the poor little pronoun assert itself and make itself heard. If there is a noun there in the nominative, the noun will always win. So be sure to search the sentence high and low before you conclude that there is no noun in the nominative; you would be amazed how easily these nouns can smuggle themselves in without your noticing them.

A noun lurking in a sentence.

A noun governing a verb.

Exercise 2.15

Copy the following sentences. Mark S for subject, V for verb and O for object and then translate them into English. Remember, only if there is no noun in the nominative case will the pronoun that is tucked up in the verb be translated.

1.   *fēminae spectant.*
2.   *fēminās spectant.*
3.   *nautās agricola laudat.*
4.   *agricolam laudant.*
5.   *puellae patriam amant.*

Exercise 2.16

Read (or sing) the following passage aloud and then answer the questions that follow.

To sing or not to sing...

1 *Cassia et Sulpicia cantant; Cassiam nauta vocat et rogat*
"Cassia, cūr cantās?" agricola Sulpiciam vocat et rogat
"cūr cantās, Sulpicia?" Cassia <u>nōn iam</u> cantat. nauta
<u>iterum</u> Cassiam vocat; Cassiam nauta, <u>quod nōn iam</u>
5 *cantat, laudat. Sulpicia <u>nōn iam</u> cantat. Sulpiciam*
agricola vocat et agricola fēminam, <u>quod nōn iam</u>
cantat, laudat. <u>intrat</u> poēta; Sulpiciam poēta et Cassiam
vocat; puellam et fēminam poēta rogat: "cūr nōn
cantātis?" Cassia et Sulpicia iterum cantant; nōn laudat
10 *nauta puellam; agricola fēminam nōn laudat; poēta*
<u>tamen</u> puellam et fēminam laudat.

nōn iam = no longer
iterum = again

quod = because
intrō = I enter

tamen = however

1. Translate the passage.

2. Answer the following questions:
   (a) *cantās* and *rogat* (line 2): give the 1st person singular of these verbs.
   (b) In line 3, what case is *Sulpicia*?
   (c) *Cassia* (line 3): give the accusative singular of this noun.
   (d) *poēta* (line 7): what is the vocative plural of this noun?
   (e) In lines 8-9 the poet asks the girl and woman why they are not singing. What change to the verb *cantātis* would be necessary if the poet were addressing the girl only?

Vocabulary 2

agricola, m.	=	farmer	*īnsula*, f.	=	island
ancilla, f.	=	maid-servant	*nauta*, m.	=	sailor
aqua, f.	=	water	*nōn*	=	not
dea, f. (irreg.) *	=	goddess	*patria*, f.	=	fatherland
etiam	=	even, also	*poēta*, m.	=	poet
fēmina, f.	=	woman	*puella*, f.	=	girl
fīlia, f. (irreg.) *	=	daughter	*quis?*	=	who?
hasta, f.	=	spear	*sagitta*, f.	=	arrow
hīc	=	here	*sed*	=	but
incola, c.**	=	inhabitant	*ubi?*	=	where?

N.B. *dea* and *fīlia* become irregular in the plural (i.e. they do slightly odd things). There's always a catch somewhere. In the dative and ablative plural they go *deābus* and *fīliābus*. Don't worry about it for now, but we thought you ought to know.

Note also that *incola* is a slippery one: it can be masculine *or* feminine. Such nouns are called common (c.) – a little snobbish, I fear.

And here ends this second chapter.

Chapter 3

More about nouns

It is now time to learn about the other three cases. We know what the nominative, vocative and accusative cases do, but the other three remain a closely guarded secret. Well, not for long!

Study once more our beautiful table for *puella* = a girl. This time we have added an extra column to the right, telling you how the six cases are used. You already know about the nominative, vocative and accusative cases, so now prepare to learn about the final three cases.

	Singular	Plural	
Nominative	*puella*	*puellae*	Subject
Vocative	*puella*	*puellae*	Addressing
Accusative	*puellam*	*puellās*	Object
Genitive	*puellae*	*puellārum*	Of
Dative	*puellae*	*puellīs*	To, for
Ablative	*puellā*	*puellīs*	With, by, from

The genitive case

The genitive case means "of".

E.g.   *filia **agricolae*** = "the daughter **of the farmer**"; or "**the farmer's** daughter."

Note that the genitive case in Latin can come before or after the noun that belongs to it. Thus:

   *filia **agricolae*** and ***agricolae** filia*

both mean "the daughter of the farmer" (or "the farmer's daughter").

Using apostrophes

As you can see, we have a genitive case of our own in English, using the apostrophe.

E.g.   *agricolae filia* = "the daughter of the farmer" or "the farmer's daughter".

Do please remember how the apostrophe works in English:

- The apostrophe comes IMMEDIATELY AFTER the noun (or nouns) doing the possessing and is used in the following ways:

The <u>cat</u>'s pyjamas means the pyjamas belonging to the **cat** (singular).

The <u>cats</u>' pyjamas means the pyjamas belonging to the **cats** (plural).

<u>Marcus</u>' cat means the cat belonging to Marcus.

Exercise 3.1

Translate into Latin, taking care with the use of the apostrophes.

1. The farmer's spears.
2. The farmers' spear.
3. The farmers' spears.
4. Claudia's daughter.
5. Claudia's daughters.
6. Quintus' sons.

The dative case

The dative case means "to" or "for" and is used particularly with verbs such as *dō* = I give.

E.g. *nauta **agricolae** hastam dat* = "the sailor is giving a spear **to the farmer**".

E.g. *agricola aquam **puellīs** parat* = "the farmer is preparing water **for the girls**".

The ablative case

Finally we come to the ablative case. Unfortunately this can mean all sorts of things, the most commonly listed of which are "with", "by" or "from". However, for the moment let's content ourselves with its meaning "with" in the following sense:

*agricola nautam **hastā** necat* = the farmer is killing the sailor **with a spear**.

Remember that ***hastā*** (with a long *ā* at the end) must be ablative singular.

All the cases

We have now met all the cases and you may be wondering how on earth you will remember which is which. Well the answer is simple. All nouns use the six cases in exactly the same way, so all you have to do is learn by heart the order in which the cases come and what each case is used for. To help you with this, here are two little things to learn:

1. Order of cases

Naughty	(**N**ominative)
Vicars	(**V**ocative)
Always	(**A**ccusative)
Go	(**G**enitive)
Downstairs	(**D**ative)
Awkwardly	(**A**blative)

2. Meanings of cases

Girl	
O girl	
Girl	
Of a girl	
To or for a girl	
With, by or from a girl	

Exercise 3.2

Now, using the emboxed (I hope you like this word. I think I have made it up) table of *puella*, answer the following questions:

1. What is the nominative plural of *agricola*?
2. What is the genitive plural of *ancilla*?
3. What is the dative singular of *hasta*?
4. What is the accusative plural of *īnsula*?
5. What is the genitive singular of *fīlia*?
6. What is the ablative singular of *Sulpicia*?
7. What is the accusative singular of *Laelia*?
8. What is the dative singular of *Cassia*?
9. What is the ablative plural of *incola*?
10. What is the dative plural of *nauta*?

Exercise 3.3

Give the Latin for:

1. Of the girls
2. For a girl
3. Of the woman
4. Of the women
5. O Laelia (when we are addressing her)
6. To Sulpicia
7. Cassia (when she is the subject)
8. Cassia (when she is the object)
9. With an arrow
10. With arrows

A minor problem

It will not have escaped your attention that some of the cases in the 1st declension use the same endings.

1. The worst offender is the ending -*ae*, which could be four different cases: genitive singular, dative singular, nominative plural or vocative plural.

2. Next comes the ending -*a*. If we ignore the macron over the top of this ending in the ablative case (and the macron will not always be marked, so you cannot rely on it), the ending -*a* could be nominative singular, vocative singular or ablative singular.

3. Finally, the ending -*īs* could be dative or ablative plural.

When translating Latin, then, we sometimes have to work out which case a word is in simply from the context, and this may well mean we have to use our common sense. It is normally pretty obvious, but sometimes a sentence could equally well mean more than one thing (these things are sent to try us!).

Exercise 3.4

Translate into English. If a sentence could mean more than one thing, say so.

1. *fēminae fīliās amant.*
2. *ancillās rēgīna vocat.*
3. *agricolae nautīs hastās dant.*
4. *agricolae, puella cantat.*
5. *fābulam poētae nārrant.*
6. *ancillās rēgīnae laudant.*
7. *nautae hastās portant.*
8. *agricolārum fīliae fēstīnant.*
9. *patriam nōn amant.*
10. *nautae īnsulam habitant.*

Exercise 3.5

Read the following passage and answer the questions that follow.

The dangers of Danegeld?

1 *agricolae et nautae pugnant; agricolae hastīs et nautae sagittīs pugnant. īnsulae rēgīna agricolīs et nautīs pecūniam dat; nōn iam pugnant. Sulpicia fēmina est; Cassia puella est. agricolās et nautās spectant. mox*
5 *Sulpicia et Cassia pugnant. diū pugnant et tandem "ubi est pecūnia?" clāmat Sulpicia. "rēgīna agricolīs et nautīs pecūniam dat. etiam fēminārum rēgīna et puellārum est. fēminae tamen et puellae pecūniam rēgīna nōn dat." "rēgīna, fēminās et puellās nōn amās!" clāmat Cassia.*
10 *"nōs igitur rēgīnam nōn amāmus!"*

pecūnia, -ae, f. = money
nōn iam = no longer
mox = soon
diū = for a long time
tandem = at last
tamen = however
igitur = therefore

1. Translate the passage into beautiful English prose.

2. Give one example from the passage of the following:

    (a) a noun in the nominative singular
    (b) a noun in the nominative plural
    (c) a noun in the accusative singular
    (d) a noun in the accusative plural
    (e) a noun in the genitive singular

    (f) a noun in the genitive plural
    (g) a noun in the dative singular
    (h) a noun in the dative plural
    (i) a noun in the ablative plural
    (j) a noun in the vocative singular

A final word on the 1st declension

Now that we have learnt almost all there is to learn about the 1st declension, here is one more thing which applies not just to it but indeed to all nouns. When we list a noun in a vocabulary from now on, we should always lay it out in the following way:

>   *puella, -ae*, f. = girl.

This gives us four vital bits of information about the noun:

1. *puella*: the nominative singular form. This tells us which noun we are talking about!

2. *-ae*: a shortened form of *puellae*, the genitive singular of the noun. We will learn later how absolutely vital it is to know the genitive singular of a noun. For now, note that every single 1st declension noun in *-a* has a genitive singular ending in *-ae*.

3. f.: short for feminine. It could have been m. for masculine, or c. for common. This tells us which gender the noun is. (There are no neuter nouns in the 1st declension.)

4. girl: the meaning of the word!

In addition, if the noun is irregular in any way, we need to learn this too. Whenever you meet a noun you must always learn these bits of information about it. If you are expecting a vocabulary test (joy of joys), learn these bits of information about every noun on your list and you are sure to do well.

Exercise 3.6

Fill in the gaps in the following vocabulary list.

1.	*ancilla,*	-ae,	f.	=	____
2.	*aqua,*	__,	f.	=	water
3.	*dea,*	-ae,	__	=	goddess (irreg.)
4.	____,	-ae,	f.	=	daughter (irreg.)
5.	*hasta,*	__,	f.	=	spear
6.	____,	-ae,	f.	=	island
7.	*īra,*	-ae,	__	=	anger
8.	*patria,*	__,	f.	=	fatherland
9.	*nauta,*	-ae,	__	=	sailor
10.	*incola,*	-ae,	c.	=	____

2nd declension nouns: dominus

You may have noticed (not that one again!) that since we have been dealing with the 1st declension, we have stopped talking about the boys, whose names (you will remember) end in *-us*. Let us now put this right by plunging straight into the 2nd declension, taking *dominus* = "lord" or "master" as our model noun. Note that all 2nd declension nouns have a genitive singular ending in *-ī*.

	dominus, -ī, m. = lord, master	
	Singular	**Plural**
Nominative	*dominus*	*dominī*
Vocative	*domine*	*dominī*
Accusative	*dominum*	*dominōs*
Genitive	*dominī*	*dominōrum*
Dative	*dominō*	*dominīs*
Ablative	*dominō*	*dominīs*

Most nouns of the 2nd declension ending in *-us* are masculine. In this book you will not meet any such nouns that are not masculine, so that's a comfort.

Exercise 3.7

Using the words below, give the Latin for:

1. Of a friend
2. To the horses
3. With food
4. O Marcus!
5. O slaves!
6. The wind (acc.)
7. The walls (nom.)
8. Of the walls
9. To a horse
10. Of the slaves

Some 2nd declension nouns like *dominus*:

amīcus, -ī, m.	=	friend		*servus, -ī*, m.	=	slave
cibus, -ī, m.	=	food		*mūrus, -ī*, m.	=	wall
dominus, -ī, m.	=	master		*ventus, -ī*, m.	=	wind
equus, -ī, m.	=	horse		*Mārcus, -ī*, m.	=	Marcus

Exercise 3.8

Translate into English:

1. Marcus watches the slave.
2. The friend prepares food.
3. The maid-servant praises the master.
4. Marcus loves the maid-servant.
5. The slave is building a wall.
6. Aulus, who is watching the horses?
7. The slaves are here.
8. There are slaves here.*
9. Where is Quintus' horse?
10. Aulus, why are you not working?

***N.B.** a little thing worth knowing is that:

- *est* = he is, she is, it is or THERE IS;
- *sunt* = they are or THERE ARE.

Exercise 3.9

Read the following passage and answer the questions that follow.

Hercules' 8th labour is to tame the mares of Diomedes

1   *Diomēdēs Thrācius est; dominus equārum est.*
    Diomēdēs cibum equīs dat: puerōs puellās fēminās
    virōs, quī dominī convīvae sunt, equae dēvorant. vir
    Thrāciam intrat; Graecus est. incolās vocat et rogat "cūr
5   *convīvās equae dominī dēvorant? dominum nōn laudō;*
    dominum equārum nōn amō?" incolae "quis es?" rogant.
    "Herculēs sum" clāmat "et hīc labōrō. ubi est
    Diomēdēs?" "Diomēdēs hīc est," clāmant incolae. mox
    Herculēs dominum necat et equīs dominum dat. sīc
10   *dominum equae dēvorant et sīc Herculēs et dominum et*
    equās superat.

Diomēdēs = Diomedes
Thrācius = Thracian
equa, -ae, f. = mare
puer, -ī, m. = boy
vir, -ī, m. = man (see page 34)
quī = who
convīva, -ae, c. = guest
dēvorō = I gobble up
Thrācia, -ae, f. = Thrace
mox = soon
sīc = thus
et ... et = both ... and

N.B. Thrace is a large region to the north of Greece.

1.   Answer the following questions:
    (a) In line 1, what are we told about Diomedes?
    (b) In lines 2-3, what did Diomedes give his mares to eat?
    (c) In line 4, what did the Greek man do before asking anything?
    (d) In lines 5-6, what was his attitude to Diomedes?
    (e) In line 7, what was Hercules doing in Thrace?
    (f) In lines 8-9, what did Hercules do to Diomedes first?
    (g) In lines 9-10, what did the mares get to eat at the end of the story?

2.   Translate the passage into nice, juicy prose (I'm sorry it is such an unsavoury story).

3.   Answer the following:
    (a) *equārum* (line 1): what part of *equa* is this?
    (b) *equīs* (line 2): in what case is this word?
    (c) *rogat* (line 4): from which verb does this come?
    (d) *incolae* (line 6): in which case is this word?
    (e) Give examples from the passage of:
      (i) two accusatives singular;
      (ii) two accusatives plural.

In some versions of the story, poor old Diomedes was fed live to the mares!

Feeling scholarly?

Before we go any further...

1. The historic present

You will have noticed that the story we have just read is told throughout in the present tense although it is about the past. This sort of present tense is called a **historic present**; it makes the whole story more vivid. In English, however, it is more natural to use the past tense and you may of course do so in translating this passage. (Another reason for our using a present tense in this passage is the fact that we have not learnt any other tenses yet, but this doesn't sound quite so impressive, does it?)

2. Asyndeton

In lines 2-3 of the passage there was no punctuation or word for "and" between the nouns making up the list of people who were fed to the mares. This omission is called **asyndeton**, from a Greek word meaning "unjoined"; rather a splendid word I hope you will agree!

2nd declension nouns in -er

There is a type of 2nd declension masculine noun which ends in –er, instead of –us. For example, *puer* = boy. We needn't panic, however, because after the nominative and vocative singular, such nouns go just like *dominus*.

	puer, puerī, m. = boy	
	Singular	**Plural**
Nominative	*puer*	*puerī*
Vocative	*puer*	*puerī*
Accusative	*puerum*	*puerōs*
Genitive	*puerī*	*puerōrum*
Dative	*puerō*	*puerīs*
Ablative	*puerō*	*puerīs*

Some nouns in –er go like *puer* except that, once they get to the accusative case, they drop the "*e*" before the final "*r*" (see opposite!). Thus *magister* goes like this:

	magister, magistrī, m. = teacher, master	
	Singular	**Plural**
Nominative	*magister*	*magistrī*
Vocative	*magister*	*magistrī*
Accusative	*magistrum*	*magistrōs*
Genitive	*magistrī*	*magistrōrum*
Dative	*magistrō*	*magistrīs*
Ablative	*magistrō*	*magistrīs*

The observant among you may have wondered why there was no pretty green ending in the nominative singular for these nouns. Well, strictly speaking, *puer* and *magister* don't have endings at all in the nominative singular (no -*us*, for example); the endings only crop up once you get to the accusative. Sorry to be pedantic.

Exercise 3.10

Write out in full the following two nouns:

1. *liber, librī*, m.   =   book
2. *ager, agrī*, m.   =   field

Exercise 3.11

Translate into English:

1. *puerī mūrōs aedificant.*
2. *agricolae et nautae clāmant.*
3. *Mārce, ubi est magistrī amīcus?*
4. *fēminae puerīs cibum parant.*
5. *ancillae ventōs nōn amant.*
6. *magistrōrum equī festīnant.*
7. *poēta Cassiae librum dat.*
8. *dominī servōs hastīs necant.* (Not very nice!)
9. *agricolae equum amant.*
10. *agricolae, ubi sunt Cassia et Laelia?*

Exercise 3.12

Translate into Latin:

1. Aulus is giving water to the boy.
2. The boy and the girl are working.
3. The slaves are building a wall.
4. The poets love the goddess.
5. Cassia and Sulpicia sing to the teacher.
6. The teacher's slaves give food to the horses.
7. The masters' slaves are not working, but they are shouting.
8. The girls love Aulus' horses.
9. Quintus, where are the slaves?
10. They are not hurrying; they are walking.

Exercise 3.13

Translate into Latin these especially silly sentences:

1. Boys and girls are giving spears to maid-servants.
2. Girls and horses sing to sailors.
3. Where are the winds and the fatherlands?
4. Farmers walk and work.
5. Sailors work and walk.
6. Farmers and sailors do not walk, but they work.
7. Sailors and farmers do not work, but they walk.
8. Master, the friends of the poet are murdering the inhabitants with books.
9. There are inhabitants here.
10. There are not.

Exercise 3.14

To return to our habitual solemnity, of which English words do the following Latin ones remind us?

1. *labōrō*
2. *liber*
3. *patria*
4. *nauta*
5. *dominus*

6. *ager*
7. *equus*
8. *puer*
9. *amīcus*
10. *vocō*

Exercise 3.15

Translate into English:

1. *poētae deōs amant.*
2. *ō Mārce, ubi sunt agricolae equī?*
3. *deae incolīs aquam dant.*

4. *deārum ancillae puellae sunt.*
5. *ō fīlī*, cibus hīc est.*

***N.B.** See below.*

deus, vir, fīlius

Before we leave this chapter, here is the full declension of three 2nd declension masculine nouns, all three of which have some rather sinister tendencies. If we don't tell you about these tendencies now, they may catch you unawares later. We have given forms that are frequently used, but variations on these may be found, just to add to the sport.

	deus, deī, m. = god		*vir, -ī*, m. = man*	
	Singular	**Plural**	**Singular**	**Plural**
Nominative	*deus*	*dī*	*vir*	*virī*
Vocative	*deus*	*dī*	*vir*	*virī*
Accusative	*deum*	*deōs*	*virum*	*virōs*
Genitive	*deī*	*deōrum* (or *deum*)	*virī*	*virōrum* (or *virum*)
Dative	*deō*	*dīs*	*virō*	*virīs*
Ablative	*deō*	*dīs*	*virō*	*virīs*

*as opposed to woman

	fīlius, fīliī, m. = son	
	Singular	**Plural**
Nominative	*fīlius*	*fīliī*
Vocative	*fīlī*	*fīliī*
Accusative	*filium*	*fīliōs*
Genitive	*fīliī*	*fīliōrum*
Dative	*fīliō*	*fīliīs*
Ablative	*fīliō*	*fīliīs*

This may be a good time to tell you that 2nd declension masculine nouns in *-ius* have a genitive in *-iī* (with two "*i*"'s together), but you may also see them with just one "*i*". We shall only give the *-iī* form in this book. Problems also occur in the vocative singular, as you can see from *fīlī*, and indeed Latin names in *-ius* (such as *Lūcius* and *Amūlius*) have vocatives singular in *-ī* (e.g. *Lūcī*). As for *vir*, although (or because?) it is such a little word, it is puffed up with self-importance and is never used of anyone "ordinary". Its chief irregularity is that it ends in *-ir*.

Vocabulary 3

ager, agrī, m. = field
amīcus, -ī, m. = friend
cibus, -ī, m. = food
deus, deī, m. (irreg.) = god
dominus, -ī, m. = lord, master
equus, -ī, m. = horse
fīlius, fīliī, m. (irreg.) = son
intrō = I enter
īra, -ae, f. = anger
liber, librī, m. = book

magister, magistrī, m. = teacher, master
mūrus, -ī, m. = wall
pecūnia, -ae, f. = money
portō = I carry
puer, puerī, m. = boy
rēgīna, -ae, f. = queen
servus, -ī, m. = slave
tamen = however*
tandem = at last
vir, virī, m. (irreg.) = man (as opposed to woman)

N.B. *tamen* (= however) is generally not written as the first Latin word in a clause or sentence.

E.g.   *puer **tamen** ancillam laudat* = **However** the boy praises the maid-servant.

Meanwhile, the 3rd chapter has slipped past and you are becoming more and more professional Latin scholars by the minute.

Chapter 4

Nouns like bellum

I'm sure you remember feeling rather sorry for the neuter, which is neither masculine nor feminine. Well I don't think you should feel sorry for it. Here is *bellum*, a 2nd declension neuter noun, and just look at how it behaves (and what it means – a thoroughly nasty customer).

bellum, -ī, n. = war		
	Singular	**Plural**
Nominative	*bellum*	*bella*
Vocative	*bellum*	*bella*
Accusative	*bellum*	*bella*
Genitive	*bellī*	*bellōrum*
Dative	*bellō*	*bellīs*
Ablative	*bellō*	*bellīs*

The main thing to note here is that neuter nouns are a strangely mixed up lot, in that the endings when they are the subject are identical to the endings when they are the object. We need to be profoundly aware of this, or it could cause problems later.

Exercise 4.1

Write out in full the following nouns:

1. *verbum, -ī*, n. = word.
2. *templum, -ī*, n. = temple
3. *oppidum, -ī*, n. = town

Exercise 4.2

Translate into English. Notice how great care is needed when dealing with neuter nouns to distinguish the subject from the object.

1. *puerī templum intrant.*
2. *nautae oppida spectant.*
3. *templum deae hīc est.*
4. *oppida et templa incola spectat.*
5. *verba agricolae nōn amant.*

Exercise 4.3

Translate into Latin.

1. Quintus praises the farmers' words.
2. Marcus and the farmers are building a temple.
3. The temple is here.
4. Aulus and Laelia enter the temple.
5. Why is there a war?

Prepositions + the ablative

A preposition is a (generally) little word that stands in front of a noun and (believe it or not) governs it. You can see from this what bossy little things they are. What's more, not content with governing a noun, they are very fussy about the case into which the noun they govern should go. For example some force the nouns they govern into the accusative, others force their nouns into the ablative, and just a few do both.

We will begin with prepositions followed by the ablative:

ā (or *ab*)	(+ abl.)	=	"from" or "by"
cum	(+ abl.)	=	"with" (i.e. "together with")
dē	(+ abl.)	=	"down from" or "concerning"
ex (or *ē*)	(+ abl.)	=	"out of"
in	(+ abl.)	=	"in" or "on"

N.B. *ā* becomes *ab* before a vowel or an *h*. To tell you the truth, *ab* is also found before certain consonants, but we are not using it so in this book.

E.g. *ā templō* = from the temple.

E.g. *ab Ītaliā* = from Italy.

N.B. *ex* occurs much more frequently than *ē*, whatever the next word begins with; and in any case *ex* would *always* be found before a vowel or an *h*.

E.g. *ex Ītaliā* = out of Italy.

But also: *ex templō* = out of the temple.

A bossy preposition

Exercise 4.4

Translate into English:

1. *Gnaeus et Sextus in īnsulā sunt.*
2. *Cassia cum amīcō cantat.*
3. *puerī ab agrīs ambulant.*
4. *Laelia ā templō deae festīnat.*
5. *poēta dē puellīs cantat.*
6. *Sulpicia dē mūrō nautīs cibum dat.*
7. *Aulus in agrō labōrat.*
8. *nautae fīliī ex aquā ambulant.*
9. *puellae ab undīs festīnant.*
10. *puerī cum ancillīs nōn ambulant.*

Exercise 4.5

Translate into Latin:

1. I am walking with my* friend.
2. The sailors are hurrying down from the temple.
3. I work with the farmer.
4. O Marcus, who is walking in the water?
5. The women are hurrying out of the island.
6. The farmers are not working in the fields.
7. Boys sing about girls.
8. The maid-servants walk from the field.

* In Latin we can leave out words such as "my" or "your" if it is obvious what we mean.

Exercise 4.6

Read the following passage and answer the questions that follow:

How some horses won a war

1 *bellum est, et nautae oppidum <u>oppugnant</u>; Mārcus et*
Sextus in oppidō sunt; perīcula bellī nōn amant. scūta
portant et nautās dē mūrō spectant. mox Quīntus et
Lūcius, poētae, cum amīcīs, ex templō festīnant; poētae
5 *cum nautīs nōn pugnant: <u>proelium</u> nōn est. Mārcus et*
Sextus ā dīs <u>auxilium</u> rogant et equōs ex <u>stabulīs</u>
<u>līberant</u>; equī ex oppidō festīnant et nautās superant.
Quīntus dē bellō cantat: "nōs poētae nautās
superāmus." poētae verbīs, nōn <u>factīs</u>, pugnant!

oppugnō = I attack (a place)

proelium, -iī, n. = battle
auxilium, -iī, n. = help
stabulum, -ī, n. = stable
līberō = I set free
factum, -ī, n. = deed

N.B. Nouns in *-ium*, like nouns in *-ius*, form their genitive singular in *-iī* or in *-ī*. We shall only mention the *-iī* form in this book.

1. Answer the following:
   (a) In line 1, what is happening to the town?
   (b) In line 2, what is the attitude of Marcus and Sextus to the war?
   (c) In lines 2-3, what do they sensibly carry?
   (d) In lines 3-4, who hurry out from the temple?
   (e) In lines 4-5, how effective are they as defenders of the town?
   (f) In lines 5-6, to whom do Marcus and Sextus turn for help?
   (g) In lines 6-7, explain what Marcus and Sextus did and what effect this had.
   (h) In lines 8-9, how modest was the poet Quintus about his part in the proceedings?
   (i) In lines 8-9, what does this tell us about the poets?

2. Translate the passage into heroic English.

3. Answer the following:
   (a) *oppidum* (line 1): in which case is this noun? Why?
   (b) *perīcula* (line 2): in which case is this noun? Why?
   (c) *bellī* (line 2): in which case is this noun? What does it mean?
   (d) *scūta* (line 2): what is the nominative singular of this noun?
   (e) In line 3 we are told that Marcus and Sextus "watch the sailors from the wall". How would the word *mūrō* change if you were to say in Latin "they watch from the **walls**?"
   (f) *proelium* (line 5): in what case is this noun?
   (g) *nautās* (line 7): what does this word mean? Explain the connexion between *nautās* and the English word "nautical".
   (h) In line 7 we are told that "the horses hurry from the town". How would the word *festīnant* change if you were to say that "the horse **hurries** from the town?"
   (i) Write down and translate all the prepositions in this passage (together with the nouns they govern).

Adjectives

And now that we've got all these splendid nouns, we simply must have some adjectives to keep them happy (or sometimes to put them in their places).

The word "adjective" means "thrown at", which I have always thought rather inadequate. The function of an adjective is to describe a noun, and I suppose it's "thrown at" it because it adds something to it, thus telling us something about it. As you can see, adjectives look just like nouns; the masculine forms go like *dominus*, the feminine ones go like *puella* and the neuter ones go like *bellum*.

---

bonus, -a, -um = good

Singular

	Masculine	Feminine	Neuter
Nominative	*bonus*	*bona*	*bonum*
Vocative	*bone*	*bona*	*bonum*
Accusative	*bonum*	*bonam*	*bonum*
Genitive	*bonī*	*bonae*	*bonī*
Dative	*bonō*	*bonae*	*bonō*
Ablative	*bonō*	*bonā*	*bonō*

Plural

	Masculine	Feminine	Neuter
Nominative	*bonī*	*bonae*	*bona*
Vocative	*bonī*	*bonae*	*bona*
Accusative	*bonōs*	*bonās*	*bona*
Genitive	*bonōrum*	*bonārum*	*bonōrum*
Dative	*bonīs*	*bonīs*	*bonīs*
Ablative	*bonīs*	*bonīs*	*bonīs*

An adjective is listed in a vocabulary with the masculine, nominative singular form in full (e.g. *bonus*) followed by the feminine and neuter endings (*-a, -um*). This helps us to remember that it is an adjective and has three sets of endings.

Exercise 4.7

Give the following forms, as in the examples below.

E.g.   Masc. acc. pl. of *malus, -a, -um* = bad: *malōs*.

E.g.   Fem. nom. pl. of *bonus, -a, -um* = good: *bonae*.

1.   Masc. acc. sing. of *altus, -a, -um* = high, deep (I ask you!)
2.   Fem. dat. pl. of *fessus, -a, -um* = tired
3.   Neut. abl. sing. of *magnus, -a, -um* = big, great
4.   Masc. acc. pl. of *laetus, -a, -um* = happy
5.   Fem. gen. sing. of *novus, -a, -um* = new
6.   Neut. abl. pl. of *parvus, -a, -um* = little
7.   Masc. voc. sing. of *saevus, -a, -um* = savage
8.   Fem. acc. pl. of *tūtus, -a, -um* = safe
9.   Fem. nom. sing. of *multus, -a, -um* = much, many
10.   Masc. dat. pl. of *malus, -a, -um* = bad

Agreement of adjectives

Now for another little rule to learn by heart:

- An adjective must agree with the noun it describes in gender, number* and case.

This means that if the noun it is describing is masculine, genitive plural, the adjective must also be masculine, genitive plural. To make this happen, we have to choose the right form of the adjective from the table above, finding the right gender, case and number to "agree" with the noun.

E.g. "Of the good masters" ; masculine genitive plural.
= *bonōrum dominōrum.*

E.g. "O good master" ; masculine vocative singular.
= *ō bone domine.*

*The word number is a kind of double bluff; it is such a sensible word for what it means (i.e. singular or plural) that we can hardly believe it!

Adjectives can come either before or after the nouns they describe, but the important thing to take to heart about them is that they always, always **agree** with their noun. In short, they are real "yes men".

An adjective agreeing with a noun

A word on genders

It is easy to talk rather airily about agreeing in gender, but as we progress we shall discover that there is no obvious reason whatever why most nouns are the gender that they are. It does not require much imagination to see that a grandmother is feminine. But why is "anger" (*īra*) feminine? Why is a "word" (*verbum*) neuter? Why is a wall (*mūrus*) masculine? Now that we are learning adjectives, it is more vital than ever to know the gender of the noun with which an adjective agrees, so we have to learn the gender of every noun that comes our way.

Exercise 4.8

Translate into Latin, making sure that the adjective agrees with the noun, as in the example. To do this correctly, always work out the gender, case and number of the noun and then make sure that the adjective agrees.

E.g. Of the big horse (masc. gen. sing.) = *equī magnī.*

1. In great danger
2. Of the bad slave
3. O good sailors!
4. Out of the big island
5. For the tired farmer

6. In the great battle
7. With the good inhabitants
8. Out of the deep water
9. The angry masters (nom.)
10. The happy masters (acc.)

A word of warning

Don't be fooled by the fact that adjectives often rhyme with the nouns they describe into thinking that they always do.

E.g. *agricola bonus* = the good farmer.

E.g. *poetārum bonōrum* = of the good poets.

Follow the rules you have learnt for the agreement of adjectives and all will be well; if they rhyme, treat this as a happy bonus!

Exercise 4.9

Translate into English:

1.   *in bellīs puerī tūtī nōn sunt.*
2.   *laetī sumus; novus magister saevus nōn est.*
3.   *malōs servōs dominī bonī nōn amant.*
4.   *bone amīce, in perīculō magnō sumus.*
5.   *parvae puellae fessae sunt.*
6.   *laetae fēminae bona verba amant.*
7.   *novum templum magnum est.*
8.   *nautae fessī sunt; in undīs altīs nāvigant.*

Sum + complement

It is now vital that you understand another little grammatical rule:

● The verb "to be" is followed by a complement in the nominative case.

A complement is simply the noun or adjective which comes after the verb "to be" to tell us more about the noun that is "being"!

	S.	V.	Comp.		
E.g.	The boy	is	good	=	*puer bonus est.*

	S.	V.	Comp.		
	Cassia	is	a maid-servant	=	*Cassia ancilla est.*

Do not be tempted to use an accusative case after the verb "to be".

Be careful, of course, not to muddle up complements with compliments, particularly as they are pronounced the same. A compliment expresses polite admiration. So, to say to a girl "*pulchra es*" (you are beautiful) would be a compliment, and what is more the adjective *pulchra* would be the complement. But if she replied "*malus es*" (you are bad), the adjective *malus* would be the complement, but certainly not a compliment!

Exercise 4.10

Translate into Latin, remembering to put the complements in the nominative case.

1. The slave is bad.
2. The sailor is angry.
3. The farmers are tired.
4. The savage sailors are overcoming the boys with arrows.
5. Happy women love good maid-servants.
6. The teachers are walking down from the high temple.
7. O little boy, where are the little girls?
8. The farmers and sailors are allies in the big island.
9. Masters give much gold to good poets.
10. Lucius is the son of a good teacher.

Exercise 4.11

Of what English words do the following Latin ones remind us?

1. *novus*
2. *magnus*
3. *socius*
4. *dominus*
5. *multus*

The imperfect tense

What with all this business about nouns, adjectives and even prepositions, we seem altogether to have forgotten our verbs. So far we have only talked of the present tense. Now we must learn a new tense: the imperfect. The imperfect means "I was" doing something, or "I used to" do something, in the past. It is formed from the present stem (*amā-*) as follows:

1st person singular	*amābam*	=	I was loving / used to love
2nd person singular	*amābās*	=	you (s.) were loving / used to love
3rd person singular	*amābat*	=	he, she or it was loving / used to love
1st person plural	*amābāmus*	=	we were loving / used to love
2nd person plural	*amābātis*	=	you (pl.) were loving / used to love
3rd person plural	*amābant*	=	they were loving / used to love

Exercise 4.12

Give the Latin for:

1. I was entering.
2. You (sing.) were praising.
3. Sextus used to sail.
4. We were singing.
5. You (pl.) were carrying.
6. They used to give.*

N.B. the imperfect of *dō* is *dăbam* (*dăbās*, *dăbat* etc.) with a short *a*.

Exercise 4.13

Translate into English, using whichever form of the English verb you prefer:

1.   *magnī virī saevōs incolās necābant.*
2.   *magister bonus poētās bonōs laudābat.*
3.   *agricolae laetī in altīs agrīs stābant.*
4.   *fessae fēminae ā mūrō magnō festīnābant.*
5.   *Sextus et Gnaeus, quod malī erant, cum puellīs pugnābant.*
6.   *agricolae, quod fessī erant*, in agrīs nōn labōrābant.*
7.   *saevī nautae parvam īnsulam oppugnābant.*
8.   *puerī cum bonīs puellīs cibum portābant.*

*See below

Exercise 4.14

Translate into Latin:

1.   The sailors were sailing in deep waves.
2.   The farmers were hurrying down from the big fields.
3.   Little boys used to sing in the temple.
4.   The happy women used to praise the good girls.
5.   The inhabitants were giving food to the good messengers.
6.   The great goddess used to live in the island.
7.   The bad men were overcoming the sailors with swords.
8.   The savage slave loves money.

Imperfect of sum

Let us now learn the imperfect of *sum*, which is, of course, irregular but not as grossly so as it is in the present tense. It goes thus, rhyming rather conveniently with our new endings: *-bam, -bās, -bat* etc.

1st person singular	*eram*	=	I was*
2nd person singular	*erās*	=	you (s.) were
3rd person singular	*erat*	=	he, she or it was
1st person plural	*erāmus*	=	we were
2nd person plural	*erātis*	=	you (pl.) were
3rd person plural	*erant*	=	they were

*Note that we don't often say "I was being" etc.; we just say "I was."

Exercise 4.15

Translate into English:

1.   *agricolae equōs nōn amant.*
2.   *nautae īnsulās intrābant.*
3.   *puellae fessae erant.*
4.   *agricolae fīlius parvus erat.*
5.   *turba saeva erat.*
6.   *malī puerī in viā erant.*
7.   *rēgīna puellās laudābat.*
8.   *bonus magister puerōs laudat.*
9.   *nautae saevī agrum intrābant.*
10. *bonus dominus servōs amat.*

A little piece on translating

Try not to think of one Latin word meaning just one English word. For example, we have learnt that *magnus* = "big" but sometimes "great" is much nearer the mark. Similarly, *laetus* = "happy" but you might sometimes wish to translate it as "glad".

Exercise 4.16

Translate into Latin, remembering the words of wisdom above about translating.

1. The woman is standing in the street.
2. We love the great queen.
3. Farmers work in the fields.
4. The girls were giving food to the tired horses.
5. The boys were looking at the waters.
6. The wicked men were killing the inhabitants.
7. The sailors were not carrying swords.
8. We were praising the allies.
9. The little girls were weary.
10. The new book is large.

Exercise 4.17

Read the following passage and answer the questions that follow:

Ulysses, after the siege of Troy, returns home to Ithaca, having had many adventures on the way

1 *Ulixēs Graecus erat; Īlium diū oppugnābat; deinde diū errābat et in magnō perīculō erat; multa tamen perīcula virum nōn superābant. in saevīs et altīs undīs nāvigābat; etiam animās mortuōrum virōrum et fēminārum*
5 *mortuārum spectābat. dea Minerva virum amābat. tandem, igitur, fessus sed laetus, īnsulam suam Ithacam intrāvit; in īnsulā diū cum laetā marītā habitābat.*

Ulixēs = Ulysses
Graecus, -a, -um = Greek
Īlium, -iī, n. = Troy
deinde = next, then
errō = I wander
anima, -ae, f. = spirit, ghost
mortuus, -a, -um = dead
Minerva, -ae, f. = Minerva, goddess
   of wisdom
suus, -a, -um = his own
Ithaca, -ae, f. = the island of Ithaca
marīta, -ae, f. = wife

1. Answer the following:
   (a) In line 1, what was Ulysses doing?
   (b) In line 2, were his wanderings pleasant? Explain your answer.
   (c) In lines 2-3, what do we learn about Ulysses' character?
   (d) In line 3, did Ulysses travel by land? Explain your answer.
   (e) In lines 4-5, what (somewhat unusually) was Ulysses watching?
   (f) In line 5, who loved Ulysses?
   (g) In line 6, how is Ulysses described here?
   (h) In line 7, what do we learn about Ulysses' wife?

2. Translate the passage into adventurous English (but not too adventurous!)

3. Answer the following:
    (a) *oppugnābat* (line 1): in which tense is this verb? Put it into the plural.
    (b) *magnō perīculō* (line 2): put these words into the accusative singular.
    (c) *perīcula* (line 2): which adjective agrees with this noun? In what case and number is it?
    (d) *saevīs* (line 3): with which noun does this adjective agree?
    (e) In lines 4-5 we are told that "he was watching the ghosts of the dead". What would the word **spectābat** become if we were told that "he **is** watching the ghosts"?
    (f) *fessus* and *laetus* (line 6): give the case of these two words.
    (g) *intrāvit* (line 7): put this word into the imperfect tense.
    (h) *laetā* (line 7): with which noun does this agree?

Vocabulary 4

ā, ab (+ abl.) = from, by
altus, -a, -um = deep, high
bellum, -ī, n. = war
bonus, -a, -um = good
cum (+ abl.) = with, together with
cūr? = why?
dē (+ abl.) = down from, concerning
ex, ē (+ abl.) = out of
fessus, -a, -um = tired
in (+ abl.) = in, on

laetus, -a, -um = happy
magnus, -a, -um = big, great
malus, -a, -um = bad
multus, -a, -um = much, many
oppidum, -ī, n. = town
parvus, -a, -um = small
stō = I stand
superō = I overcome
templum, -ī, n. = temple
verbum, -ī, n. = word

And so, this is the end of Chapter 4. Be of good cheer, however; there are plenty more to come.

Chapter 5

Learning to count: I - X

It is now time to learn our numbers up to ten. Here they are in the nominative, together with the Roman numerals:

		Masculine	Feminine	Neuter
I	=	*ūnus*	*ūna*	*ūnum*
II	=	*duo*	*duae*	*duo*
III	=	*trēs*	*trēs*	*tria*
IV	=	*quattuor*		
V	=	*quīnque*		
VI	=	*sex*		
VII	=	*septem*		
VIII	=	*octō*		
IX	=	*novem*		
X	=	*decem*		

The first three numbers have different forms for masculine, feminine and neuter, and indeed they have different forms (some of which are rather exotic) for all the various cases too, but we needn't worry about that just now. However, after these sinister beginnings, the numbers suddenly repent and from *quattuor* to *decem* become indeclinable. This, delightfully, means that in all the cases they remain stubbornly the same.

Whatever you do, don't be caught out by the innocent appearance of *ūnus*. You will learn that it is a villain of the first order, and most certainly does not go like *bonus*.

Exercise 5.1

Translate into English:

1. *trēs fēminae in mūrō stant.*
2. *quattuor puerī clāmābant.*
3. *ūnus agricola equōs spectābat.*
4. *decem puellae in īnsulā habitant.*
5. *septem nautae nāvigābant.*
6. *duae ancillae dē deā cantant.*
7. *quīnque librī in templō sunt.*
8. *novem equī ex undīs ambulant.*
9. *sex virī poētam laudābant..*
10. *octō bonī servī labōrant.*

Exercise 5.2

Translate the following sums into Latin words, using *et* for + and *sunt* for =, as in the example:

E.g.   I + II = *ūnus et duo trēs sunt.*

1.   IV + V =
2.   V + III =
3.   II + IV =
4.   V + V =
5.   IV + III =

Exercise 5.3

Translate into Latin:

1.   Nine slaves were working.
2.   Ten inhabitants lived on the island.
3.   One girl stands in the field.
4.   Seven boys were singing.
5.   Two men are praising the poet.
6.   Six women were in the temple.
7.   Three horses were hurrying out of the waves.
8.   Eight horses are standing in the field.

Prepositions + the accusative

We have already met prepositons followed by the ablative case. Here now are some prepositions which govern the accusative.

ad	(+ acc.)	=	to, towards
contrā	(+ acc.)	=	against
in	(+ acc.)	=	into, on to
per	(+ acc.)	=	through, along
prope	(+ acc.)	=	near
trāns	(+ acc.)	=	across

Note how our old friend *in* re-appears here and governs the accusative as well as the ablative:

$\qquad$ *in* + acc. = into (or on to);
$\qquad$ *in* + abl. = in (or on).

Try not to muddle these two meanings. The difference looks simple enough but it is very easy to get them wrong – and they nearly always crop up in exams!

Dative of the possessor

Before we launch into our next story, here is a little thing on a use of the dative case which could catch you out if you are not careful. In Latin the dative case is used with the verb *sum* to denote the possessor:

E.g.   *puerō liber est* = there is to the boy a book; i.e. the boy has a book.

E.g.   *fēminae septem fīliī sunt* = there are to the woman seven sons; i.e. the woman has seven sons.

This will be useful in coping with the first sentence of our next story.

Exercise 5.4

Read the following passage aloud and then answer the questions that follow.

The story of Niobe

1 erant <u>Niobae</u>, septem filiī et septem filiae; ōlim sīc Nioba
  <u>iactābat</u> "Lātōnae ūnus filius et ūna filia sunt; Niobae
  septem filiae cum septem filiīs sunt." Lātōna,
  magnopere īrāta erat. filius Lātōnae Phoebus Apollō erat
5 et filia Dĭāna*. Phoebus Apollō septem filiōs Niobae
  sagittīs necat et sīc Dĭāna filiās necat. tandem <u>ventī</u>
  Niobam per caelum ad <u>Sipylum</u> portant. ibi Nioba
  <u>saxum</u> est et in <u>oculīs</u> <u>saxī</u> semper aqua est; Nioba
  semper <u>lacrimat</u>.

Nioba : Niobe
iactō = I boast
ventus, -ī, m. = wind
Sipylus, -ī, m. : a mountain in Asia Minor
saxum, -ī, n. = rock
oculus, -ī, m. = eye
lacrimō = I weep

***N.B.** Diana was the goddess of hunting. Her name could be pronounced Dĭāna or Dīāna; in other words the i could be pronounced long or short. Apollo was, among other things, the god of light and prophecy.

1. Answer the following questions:
   (a) In line 1, how many children did Niobe have?
   (b) In line 2, how many children did Latona have?
   (c) In lines 4-5, why was it rash for Niobe to compare herself with Latona?
   (d) In lines 6-7, what happened to Niobe after the death of her children?
   (e) In lines 7-8, what did she become?

2. Translate this passage sadly.

3. Answer the following questions:
   (a) *sunt* (line 3): why is this plural verb used here?
   (b) *sagittīs* (line 6): in what case is this noun and what does it mean?
   (c) *filiās* (line 6): in what case is this noun and what does it mean?
   (d) In lines 6-7 we are told that "the winds carry Niobe through the sky". What change would be necessary to the word *portant* if we were to say "the wind **carries** Niobe through the sky"?
   (e) In lines 8-9 we are told that Niobe "is crying". What change to the word *lacrimat* would be necessary if we were to say that she "**was crying**"?

The perfect tense

And now comes something really encouraging. We have recently talked about the imperfect tense and have taken great care not to make too much of its obviously low status. Well, now we can turn away from this sad situation and come to a very different tense – the perfect. This tense of *amō* means "I have loved" or "I loved" and goes as follows:

1st person singular	*amāvī*	=	I have loved or I loved
2nd person singular	*amāvistī*	=	you (s.) have loved or you loved
3rd person singular	*amāvit*	=	he, she or it has loved or he, she or it loved
1st person plural	*amāvimus*	=	we have loved or we loved
2nd person plural	*amāvistis*	=	you (pl.) have loved or you loved
3rd person plural	*amāvērunt*	=	they have loved or they loved

The endings for this tense (*-ī, -istī, -it, -imus, -istis, -ērunt*) are added on to something called the perfect stem, in this case *amāv-*. All verbs have a perfect stem and you will not be surprised to hear that this is another thing you will be expected to learn by heart – hooray! For now, though, all you need to know is that most verbs like *amō* change the *-ō* to *-āv* and then add the endings. Easy!

Needless to say, two very important verbs, *dō* and *stō*, have quite preposterously irregular perfect stems: *dō* goes *ded-* and *stō* goes *stet-*. But having learnt this fact, fear not, as the tenses themselves go along in a perfectly acceptable way (*dedī, dedistī, dedit*, etc.; *stetī, stetistī, stetit*, etc.)

Note that although we have given two meanings for this tense, namely "have loved" and " loved", it is only a true perfect tense when the "have loved" meaning is used. The other meaning is a **simple past** tense, but as the latter has no distinct form in Latin, we can refer to this tense as the perfect without upsetting too many people.

Exercise 5.5

Translate into English, using *both* English translations of the perfect tense where appropriate.

E.g. *ambulāvit* = he has walked or he walked.

1. *ex templō Aulus ambulāvit.*
2. *Gnaeus et Sextus in undās festīnāvērunt.*
3. *ubi sunt puerī? templum intrāvērunt.*
4. *agricolae in agrīs labōrāvērunt.*
5. *ubi sunt nautae? ad īnsulam nāvigāvērunt.*
6. *Sulpicia et Cassia cantāvērunt.*

Exercise 5.6

Translate into Latin:

1. Where are the sailors? They have sailed across the waves.
2. We have hurried through the large field.
3. You (plural) praised the poets.
4. They carried many books into the temple.
5. You (singular) have sung.
6. You (singular) sang.

Adjectives in -er

Just as some 2nd declension nouns end in *-er* (e.g. *puer, magister* etc.), some adjectives do as well. This is not a problem. Just treat them as you treated *puer* and *magister* and all will be well.

miser, -a, -um = wretched, unhappy

Singular

	Masculine	Feminine	Neuter
Nominative	*miser*	*misera*	*miserum*
Vocative	*miser*	*misera*	*miserum*
Accusative	*miserum*	*miseram*	*miserum*
Genitive	*miserī*	*miserae*	*miserī*
Dative	*miserō*	*miserae*	*miserō*
Ablative	*miserō*	*miserā*	*miserō*

Plural

	Masculine	Feminine	Neuter
Nominative	*miserī*	*miserae*	*misera*
Vocative	*miserī*	*miserae*	*misera*
Accusative	*miserōs*	*miserās*	*misera*
Genitive	*miserōrum*	*miserārum*	*miserōrum*
Dative	*miserīs*	*miserīs*	*miserīs*
Ablative	*miserīs*	*miserīs*	*miserīs*

This type of adjective "keeps its *e*", as *puer* did. But there is another type of adjective which "drops its *e*", as *magister* did:

pulcher, pulchra, pulchrum = beautiful

Singular

	Masculine	Feminine	Neuter
Nominative	*pulcher*	*pulchra*	*pulchrum*
Vocative	*pulcher*	*pulchra*	*pulchrum*
Accusative	*pulchrum*	*pulchram*	*pulchrum*
Genitive	*pulchrī*	*pulchrae*	*pulchrī*
Dative	*pulchrō*	*pulchrae*	*pulchrō*
Ablative	*pulchrō*	*pulchrā*	*pulchrō*

Plural

	Masculine	Feminine	Neuter
Nominative	*pulchrī*	*pulchrae*	*pulchra*
Vocative	*pulchrī*	*pulchrae*	*pulchra*
Accusative	*pulchrōs*	*pulchrās*	*pulchra*
Genitive	*pulchrōrum*	*pulchrārum*	*pulchrōrum*
Dative	*pulchrīs*	*pulchrīs*	*pulchrīs*
Ablative	*pulchrīs*	*pulchrīs*	*pulchrīs*

See how the *e* has fallen right out by the time we get to the accusative singular?

Exercise 5.7

Read the following passage aloud and then answer the questions that follow.

Pluto carries off Proserpina

1   *Cerēs dea est. fīlia deae Prōserpina est; Prōserpina*
puella bona et pulchra et laeta erat. ōlim in agrīs cum
<u>amīcīs</u> ambulābat. Plūtō deus, <u>Tartarī</u> dominus, puellās
spectābat et Prōserpinam amāvit. puellam deus in
5   *<u>Tartarum</u> portāvit; ibi Prōserpina rēgīna erat. Tartarus*
tamen <u>locus</u> bonus nōn erat sed malus et saevus.
Prōserpina <u>igitur</u>, <u>quod</u> pulchrōs agrōs et terram laetam
et bonōs ventōs amābat, ibi misera erat.

amīca, -ae, f. = girl-friend
Tartarus, -ī, m. = the Underworld

locus, -ī, m. = place
igitur = therefore
quod = because

1.   Answer the following questions:
(a) What do we learn about Proserpina in lines 1-2?
(b) Who was Pluto (line 3)?
(c) What was Pluto doing in lines 3-4?
(d) In lines 4-5 what two further things do we learn about Pluto?
(e) Why was Proserpina so unhappy in the Underworld (lines 5-6)?

2.   Translate the passage into ominous English.

3.   Answer the following:
(a) *Tartarī* (line 3): in which case is this word?
(b) *amāvit* and *portāvit* (lines 4-5): in which tense are these verbs?
(c) *puellam* (line 4): in which case is this word?
(d) *rēgīna* (line 5): in which case is this word?
(e) Write down and translate all the examples of prepositions followed by their cases.
(f) Write down and translate all the verbs in the imperfect tense.
(g) *pulchrōs agrōs* (line 7): what would be the nominative singular of this phrase?
(h) *misera* (line 8): what would be the nominative feminine plural form of this adjective?

Exercise 5.8

Which English words do the following Latin ones remind you of?

1. *puer*
2. *magister*
3. *locus*
4. *miser*
5. *ventus*
6. *contrā*

Perfect of sum

The verb *sum*, which you know is irregular, has a rather glorious perfect tense. The endings are exactly the same as all other perfect tense endings, but it has a very odd-looking stem:

1st person singular	*fuī*	=	I have been or I was
2nd person singular	*fuistī*	=	you (s.) have been or you were
3rd person singular	*fuit*	=	he, she or it has been or was
1st person plural	*fuimus*	=	we have been or we were
2nd person plural	*fuistis*	=	you (pl.) have been or you were
3rd person plural	*fuērunt*	=	they have been or they were

Exercise 5.9

Translate into English:

1. *Aulus et amīcī, ubi labōrant, saepe cantant.*
2. *Claudia et Cassia, ubi labōrāvērunt, laetae erant.*
3. *etiam agricolae cantābant.*
4. *mox incolae poētis multum aurum dedērunt.*
5. *poētae igitur laetī fuērunt.*
6. *itaque poētae laetī fuērunt.*
7. *fessae ancillae diū ambulābant.*
8. *saevī nautae statim cum incolīs pugnāvērunt.*
9. *deinde rēgīna fēminās iterum laudābat.*
10. *ibi bonus dominus servīs bonum cibum dabat.*

Exercise 5.10

Translate into Latin:

1. The girl loves the horse.
2. The sailor has called the woman.
3. The farmer watched the field.
4. A slave is building a big wall.
5. The goddess loves the man.
6. The master was carrying gold into the temple.
7. You (s.) used to work in the fields.
8. We were attacking the town.
9. The teacher has praised the boy.
10. The goddess inhabits the sky.

Exercise 5.11

Read through the following piece carefully, and then answer the questions that follow it.

A horse is rescued

1 ōlim in īnsulā saevī incolae hastīs equum necāre
temptābant. Mārcus et Sextus, quod equum amābant, in
templum festīnāvērunt, et ubi in templō fuērunt, ā deō
auxilium rogāvērunt. "ō deus", clāmāvērunt, "auxilium
5 contrā malōs incolās rogāmus". deus bonus erat et
validus, et puerīs vīnum dedit; puerī incolīs vīnum
dedērunt et sīc incolās superāvērunt. et ubi puerī vīnō
incolās superāvērunt, equus tūtus erat.

temptō = I try
ubi = when

1. Answer the following:
   (a) In line 1 how is the horse being attacked?
   (b) In lines 2-3 what did Marcus and Sextus do?
   (c) Why did they do this?
   (d) In lines 5-6 how is the god described?
   (e) In lines 7-8 with what did the boys overcome the inhabitants?
   (f) How do you think it did the trick?
   (g) In line 8 how did the horse end up?

2. Translate the passage into horsey English

3. Answer the following:
   (a) In lines 2-3 what does *in templum* mean?
   (b) In line 3 what does *in templō* mean? (Didn't I warn you that this would keep cropping up?)
   (c) In line 3 what is the tense of *festīnāvērunt?*
   (d) In line 4 what is the case of *deus*?
   (e) In line 5 in what case is *malōs,* and why?
   (f) In line 5 what is the case of *deus?*
   (g) In line 6 what is the case of *puerīs?*
   (h) In line 8 what tense is *superāvērunt?*

Coping with principal parts

We now need to fill in a vital point about verbs which we have been hiding from you. To put it bluntly: verbs have principal parts, quite a noble name for once. And it makes quite good sense too because once you know a verb's principal parts, you can work out from them everything you need to know about that verb.

There are four principal parts:

1. the 1st person singular of the present tense: e.g. *amō*
2. the present infinitive: e.g. *amāre*
3. the 1st person singular of the perfect tense: e.g. *amāvī*
4. and finally the supine: e.g. *amātum*

And, of course, it's all useless unless you add the meaning in English. So this is the way a Latin verb should be presented:

> *amō, amāre, amāvī, amātum* = I love.

The 1st principal part tells us which verb we are handling.

The 2nd principal part is the present infinitive, meaning "to love" (or "to fight", or "to" whatever the verb happens to be). The present infinitive, as well as being useful in its own right, tells us to which conjugation a verb belongs (there are four main conjugations in Latin, so this is very important).

The 3rd principal part tells us how the perfect tense of the verb begins. Indeed, were we to chop off the letter -*ī*, we would have the perfect stem of the verb (hooray).

The 4th principal part is the supine. This is rather a weird customer; the word supine means "lying on one's back" and the supine is so lazy that it is hardly ever used. So why, you ask, is it one of the principal parts? The reason is that, although the supine itself is rare, there are two forms derived from it which are immensely frequent. Another reason for being interested in the supine is the fact that lots and lots of English words are derived from it. This we shall soon see.

The majority of verbs that go like *amō* have principal parts that copy the pattern of *amō* exactly. Here, for example, are the principal parts of *labōrō*:

> *labōrō, labōrāre, labōrāvī, labōrātum* = I work.

Exercise 5.12

Write out the principal parts of the following verbs (they all behave nicely), not forgetting their meanings.

1. *vocō*
2. *clāmō*
3. *aedificō*
4. *ambulō*
5. *pugnō*

N.B. Just occasionally you will meet a 1st conjugation verb that behaves badly. For example, the verb *dō* (= I give) has the following principal parts:

> *dō dăre dedī dătum* = I give.

Not only is that perfect tense (*dedī*) odd, to put it mildly, as we saw when we met it earlier, but the "*a*"s in *dare* and *datum* that are normally so beautifully long in this conjugation, are absurdly short. *Stō* is another baddy, going *stō, stāre, stetī, stătum*.

Exercise 5.13

Give all four principal parts and the meaning of the verbs from which the following forms come:

1. *aedificāre*
2. *labōrāvī*
3. *vocātum*
4. *cantō*
5. *necāre*

Using those supines

We have said that you will not be using the supine of a verb for some time to come. However, until that exciting time comes, there is something that you can do with a supine which can fill the long winter evenings and help with your English vocabulary too. If you take a supine, chop off the *-um* and add *-ion*, you very often get an English word. Try this with *vocātum* (the supine of *vocō*): you get vocation. Try it with *habitātum* (the supine of *habitō*); you get habitation. This trick gets more and more useful as we learn more Latin verbs, so store it up for future use.

Vocabulary 5			
ad (+ acc.)	= to, towards	*ūnus, -a, -um* (irreg.)	= one
contrā (+ acc.)	= against	*duo, duae, duo* (irreg.)	= two
in (+ acc.)	= into, on to	*trēs, trēs, tria* (irreg.)	= three
per (+ acc.)	= through, along	*quattuor*	= four
trāns (+ acc.)	= across	*quīnque*	= five
īrātus, -a, -um	= angry	*sex*	= six
Rōmānus, -a, -um	= Roman	*septem*	= seven
miser, misera, miserum	= unhappy	*octō*	= eight
pulcher, pulchra, pulchrum	= beautiful	*novem*	= nine
sacer, sacra, sacrum	= sacred	*decem*	= ten

Sadly, we are now over half way through this joyful ride. But fear ye not, there are plenty more goodies to come.

Chapter 6

2nd conjugation: moneō

Now that you know so much about *amō* and the verbs that go like it, it is time to meet another type of verb. We will set it out in the three tenses that you have met. From now on we will only give one meaning for each tense. Check back to our work on *amō* if you can't remember the other possible meanings.

---

moneō, monēre, monuī, monitum = I warn / advise

Present tense

1st person singular	*moneō*	=	I warn
2nd person singular	*monēs*	=	you (s.) warn
3rd person singular	*monet*	=	he, she or it warns
1st person plural	*monēmus*	=	we warn
2nd person plural	*monētis*	=	you (pl.) warn
3rd person plural	*monent*	=	they warn

Imperfect tense

1st person singular	*monēbam*	=	I was warning
2nd person singular	*monēbās*	=	you (s.) were warning
3rd person singular	*monēbat*	=	he, she, it was warning
1st person plural	*monēbāmus*	=	we were warning
2nd person plural	*monēbātis*	=	you (pl.) were warning
3rd person plural	*monēbant*	=	they were warning

Perfect tense

1st person singular	*monuī*	=	I have warned
2nd person singular	*monuistī*	=	you (s.) have warned
3rd person singular	*monuit*	=	he, she, it has warned
1st person plural	*monuimus*	=	we have warned
2nd person plural	*monuistis*	=	you (pl.) have warned
3rd person plural	*monuērunt*	=	they have warned

As you can see, in the present and imperfect tense *moneō* uses exactly the same endings as *amō* but, instead of having a present stem ending in *-ā/a*, it has one ending in *-ē/e*.

The perfect tense endings (*-ī, -istī, -it, -imus, -istis, -ērunt*) are the same for all verbs. The regular formation for the perfect tense for this conjugation sees *-eō* change to *-uī*, but, as you will soon discover, many verbs do not toe the line on this one.

More on principal parts

Now that you have met these little fellows, you need to start using them properly. We now know that the 2nd principal part tells us to which conjugation a verb belongs. Verbs in *-āre* go like *amō*, verbs in *-ēre* go like *moneō*. So far so good. But we also need to be alert for that 3rd principal part, because it shows us how the perfect tense goes. We have already said that many verbs like *moneō* go *-uī* in the perfect, but many do not, so:

● when you learn a new verb, always, always learn its principal parts.

You won't be needing the supine for some time yet, but take it from me, it has to be learnt eventually and it is easier to learn it now than to come back for it later!

Exercise 6.1

Study the verbs in the vocabulary below. Now write out the following tenses:

1. Present tense of *dēleō*
2. Imperfect tense of *timeō*
3. Perfect tense of *teneō*

4. Present tense of *videō*
5. Imperfect tense of *respondeō*
6. Perfect tense of *moveō*

dēleō, -ēre, dēlēvī, dēlētum	=	I destroy
teneō, -ēre, tenuī, tentum	=	I hold
habeō, -ēre, habuī, habitum	=	I have
terreō, -ēre, terruī, territum	=	I frighten
iubeō, -ēre, iussī, iussum	=	I order
timeō, -ēre, timuī*	=	I fear
maneō, -ēre, mānsī, mānsum	=	I remain, stay
videō, -ēre, vīdī, vīsum	=	I see
moveō, -ēre, mōvī, mōtum	=	I move (transitive)
respondeō, -ēre, respondī, respōnsum	=	I reply
rīdeō, -ēre, rīsī, rīsum	=	I laugh

*Note that it is possible for a verb not to have a 4th principal part. When you meet such a beast, learn the fact that it has no 4th principal part as soundly as you would have learnt the part itself.

Exercise 6.2

Using the trick we learnt on page 55 for finding an English word in -ion from the supine of a Latin verb, give an English word from the following and explain the connexion between the word you find and the Latin verb from which it is formed.

1. *dēlētum*
2. *mānsum*
3. *vīsum*
4. *mōtum*
5. *statum*

Exercise 6.3

Translate into English:

1. *dominī incolās dē bellō monent.*
2. *magister puerum respondēre iubet.*
3. *servī scūta in agrōs movent.*
4. *Cassia poētam timet.*
5. *Aulus, vir validus, puerōs nōn timet.*
6. *Sulpicia et Laelia, magistrī fīliae, perterritae erant.*
7. *parvae puellae pulchrōs librōs habent.*
8. *cibum Lūciō, bonō puerō, dedērunt.*

Exercise 6.4

Read the following passage aloud and answer the questions that follow:

Laurelus and Hardius attempt to move a statue

1 *Laurelus et Hardius, amīcī, saevum dominum habuērunt. dominus amīcōs <u>statuam</u> pulchram et magnam et altam ex oppidō in templum movēre iussit; amīcī statuam saepe <u>sublevāre</u> <u>temptābant</u>, sed <u>frūstrā</u>. duae puellae,*

5 *Sulpicia et Laelia, amīcōs dē īrā dominī monuērunt et amīcōs, quod dominum magnopere timēbant, terruērunt. videt dominus īrātus amīcōs et clāmat: "cūr statuam nōn <u>sublevāvistis?</u>" nōn respondent. iterum et iterum statuam <u>sublevāre</u> <u>temptant</u>, sed statua semper in suō locō*

10 *manet. subitō statuam <u>sublevant</u> et statim nōn iam tenent; statua ad terram <u>volat. heu!</u> amīcī statuam dēlēvērunt. dominus clāmat; Sulpicia et Laelia rīdent.*

statua, -ae, f. = statue

sublevō, -āre = I lift
temptō, -āre = I try
frūstrā = in vain

volō, -āre = I fly
heu = alas

1.   Answer the following questions:
      (a) In line 1, what sort of master did the two friends have?
      (b) In lines 2-3, what were the two ordered to do?
      (c) In lines 4-5, what did Sulpicia and Laelia warn them about?
      (d) In line 6, how did this affect them?
      (e) In lines 7-8, what are we told the master did?
      (f) In lines 9-10, how successful were the friends in their first attempts to move the statue?
      (g) In lines 11-12 what happened to the statue?

2.   Translate the passage into English prose (tragic or otherwise).

3.   Answer the following questions:
      (a) *dominum* (line 1): Explain the connexion between *dominus* and the English word dominate.
      (b) Write down all the adjectives in this passage and say for each one which noun it agrees with.
      (c) Write down and translate an infinitive from this passage.
      (d) In line 7 we are told that "the master sees the friends". What change to the word **videt** would be necessary if we were to say "the master **has seen** the friends"?
      (e) *respondent* (line 8): put this verb into the perfect tense.
      (f) In line 10 we are told that "the statue stays in its place". What change to the word **manet** would be necessary if we were to say "the statue **was staying** in its place".
      (g) *rīdent* (line 12): put this verb into the perfect tense.

Apposition

And now for a little word on something called **apposition**. When we say, for example, "I led Julia, my friend, into the street", we are using apposition. The words "my friend" are in apposition to "Julia" and, because they explain or describe her, **must go into the same case** as she does.

E.g.   *Iūliam, amīcam meam, in viam dūcēbam* = I was leading Julia, my friend, into the street.
       Aulus, amīcus meus, in agrōs ambulāvit = Aulus, my friend, walked into the fields.

Exercise 6.5

Translate into Latin, keeping an eye out for apposition as you go:

1.   The farmers destroyed the shields.
2.   Claudia, the master's daughter, is remaining in the town.
3.   We, the poet's sons, are laughing.
4.   You sailors fear savage waves.
5.   Good horses do not frighten little girls.
6.   We are happy because we have good books.
7.   I gave a book to Aulus, Quintus' son.
8.   They are ordering the slaves to hurry.

Pronouns in the accusative

Remember the pronouns *ego, tū, nōs, vōs*? Well it's time to say a bit more about these. Pronouns are almost nouns, and decline, even as nouns do (but in their own way). For the moment we will be content with their nominative and accusative forms only:

	Nom.		**Acc.**	
1st person	*ego*	I	*mē*	me
2nd person	*tū*	you (sing.)	*tē*	you (sing.)
1st person	*nōs*	we	*nōs*	us
2nd person	*vōs*	you (pl.)	*vōs*	you (pl.)

Exercise 6.6

Translate the following sentences into English:

1. *puella mē terruit.*
2. *agricola tē monuit.*
3. *nautae mē festīnāre iussērunt.*
4. *ego tē amō.*
5. *tū mē nōn amās.*

Exercise 6.7

Translate the following sentences into English:

1. *puerī patriam amant.*
2. *agricola suīs servīs, quod in agrō labōrāvērunt, pecūniam dedit.*
3. *agricola nōs timuit.*
4. *dominī servōs bonōs terruit.*
5. *in templō deae multum aurum erat.*
6. *puerī, ubi dē mūrō festīnāvērunt, rīsērunt.*
7. *nōs labōrāmus et vōs spectāmus.*
8. *puellae equōs vīdērunt.*

Exercise 6.8

Translate into Latin:

1. They are destroying the wall.
2. The farmer sees the field.
3. The boy holds a book
4. The master has many friends.
5. Danger was frightening the horse.
6. Sulpicia and Cassia fear war.
7. The sailor was laughing.
8. You (pl.) are advising me.

Exercise 6.9

Of what English words do the following Latin words remind us?

1. *dēleō*
2. *respondeō*
3. *terreō*
4. *timeō*
5. *moneō*

Exercise 6.10

Translate into English:

1. *puerī nōn hīc sunt, sed ibi.*
2. *agricolae numquam cum nautīs in templō pugnābant.*
3. *puellae ad templum tandem festīnābant.*
4. *puerī tamen nōn festīnant. ubi sunt?*
5. *quīnque equōs in agrōs agricola mōvit.*
6. *puerī, quod timēbant, magistrō non respondēbant.*
7. *vōs labōrātis et nōs spectātis.*
8. *incolās in oppidō manēre iubēs.*

Exercise 6.11

Translate into Latin:

1. The boy is moving the book.
2. The woman is warning the girl.
3. The maid-servant was watching the beautiful queen.
4. The teacher praises the poet.
5. The angry man is holding a sword.
6. The farmers were remaining in the fields.
7. We are hurrying out of the waves.
8. The wicked men have frightened the inhabitants.

Questions in Latin

et tū, Brūte?

Here are two ways of asking a question in Latin.

1. We can use a questioning word:

ubi	=	where?
cūr	=	why?
quis	=	who?
quid	=	what?

E.g.   *ubi est puella?* = where is the girl?
       cūr pugnās? = why are you fighting?

2. We can add *-ne* to the first word in the sentence and, hey-presto, there you are.

E.g.   *cantatne puella?* = is the girl singing?
       agricolaene pugnant? = are the farmers fighting?

Of course it is also possible to ask a question simply by changing the tone of one's voice, as Julius Caesar famously demonstrated with the immortal (excuse the irony!) words: *et tū, Brūte?*

Actually, he said this in Greek, but you get the point, don't you!

Exercise 6.12

Translate the following questions:

1. *ambulantne in viā puerī?*
2. *portantne fēminae aquam?*
3. *parantne ancillae cibum?*
4. *equōsne timent nautae?*
5. *ubi sunt Mārcus et Quīntus?*

6. *quis magistrōs vīdit?*
7. *quid spectābant virī?*
8. *cūr timētis?*
9. *puellaene in agrīs rīdēbant?*
10. *clāmantne in agrīs puerī?*

Exercise 6.13

Read the following piece carefully, and then answer the questions that follow:

Some sailors arrive at an island, seeking gold

1 *multī nautae, ubi incolae in agrīs labōrant, ad īnsulam nāvigant. "ubi est aurum vestrum?" clāmant et, ubi incolae nōn respondent, iterum clāmant "ubi est aurum vestrum?" et incolās gladiīs et hastīs terrent. tandem,*
5 *perterritī incolae "in oppidō nostrō est" respondent. itaque nautae, propter verba incolārum laetī, in oppidum festīnant.*

propter (+ acc.) = because of

1. Answer the following questions:
   (a) In lines 1-2 what are the sailors doing?
   (b) In line 1 what are the inhabitants doing?
   (c) In line 2 what do the sailors want to know?
   (d) In line 3 which Latin word shows that they wouldn't take "no" for an answer?
   (e) In line 4 what do the sailors do?
   (f) In lines 6-7, why do the sailors hurry into the town?

2. Translate the passage into exciting English.

3. Answer the following:
   (a) *īnsulam* (line 1): in which case is this word? Why?
   (b) *nāvigant* (line 2): put this verb into the imperfect tense.
   (c) *respondent* (line 3): put this verb into the perfect tense.
   (d) *terrent* (line 4): put this verb into the imperfect tense.
   (e) *in oppidō* (line 5): what case is *oppidō*? Translate the phrase.
   (f) *in oppidum* (line 6): what case is *oppidum*? Translate the phrase.

I'm sure you're all agog to know what happens next. However, for the moment, you must be patient, and look forward to the exciting sequel.

3rd conjugation: regō

And now for our third type of verb, the 3rd conjugation. Some of you may have heard on the grape-vine that *regō* is a pig, and generally does things to upset us, and I regret to say that this is true.

---

regō, regere, rēxī, rēctum = I rule

Present tense

1st person singular	*regō*	=	I rule
2nd person singular	*regis*	=	you (s.) rule
3rd person singular	*regit*	=	he, she or it rules
1st person plural	*regimus*	=	we rule
2nd person plural	*regitis*	=	you (pl.) rule
3rd person plural	*regunt*	=	they rule

Imperfect tense

1st person singular	*regēbam*	=	I was ruling
2nd person singular	*regēbās*	=	you (s.) were ruling
3rd person singular	*regēbat*	=	he, she, it was ruling
1st person plural	*regēbāmus*	=	we were ruling
2nd person plural	*regēbātis*	=	you (pl.) were ruling
3rd person plural	*regēbant*	=	they were ruling

Perfect tense

1st person singular	*rēxī*	=	I have ruled
2nd person singular	*rēxistī*	=	you (s.) have ruled
3rd person singular	*rēxit*	=	he, she, it has ruled
1st person plural	*rēximus*	=	we have ruled
2nd person plural	*rēxistis*	=	you (pl.) have ruled
3rd person plural	*rēxērunt*	=	they have ruled

There is quite a lot to say about this:

1.   The present stem of *regō* is *reg-*, to which we add the endings *-o, -is, -it, -imus, -itis, -unt*.

2.   The present infinitive of *regō* is *regere* with a short *e* in the middle, not to be mixed up with that of *moneō* which is *monēre* with a long *ē*. This means that, with any verb ending in consonant + *ō*, you must immediately learn its present infinitive. Indeed, if you don't form this habit from an early age, you will, alas!, (note 'will' not 'may') come to grief. For example, given only *dūcō* and *rogō*, you can't tell to which conjugation either of these belongs (it could be 1st, like *amō*; it could be 3rd like *regō*); but as soon as you know the present infinitives, namely *dūcere* and *rogāre*, all is well.

3.   There is no reliable pattern to the last two principal parts of verbs like *regō* and they just have to be learnt. Sorry.

So far we've had lots and lots of rules, and perhaps we haven't been as grateful for them as we ought to have been. Just think for one more moment how much worse it is not to have any rules. And this is precisely what happens when we come to the perfect of the 3rd conjugation. There is no rule to help you to form this tense, only at its best a sort of *feel* for how it might go.

A horrible truth

To continue on this line, we have gradually been breaking a horrible truth to you, but for those of you with a slightly insensitive nature, let us now make it absolutely blunt and clear. Stiffen your upper lip and be prepared. For although some verbs follow a regular pattern in the way they form their principal parts and thus their tenses, many, many verbs do not. And while the majority of verbs of the 1st conjugation have principal parts going -*ō*, -*āre*, -*āvī*, -*ātum*, and a good many 2nd conjugation ones go -*eō*, -*ēre*, -*uī*, -*itum*, we now know quite enough to realise that there will be all sorts of horrors to cope with. How on earth, for example, were we supposed to know that *iussī* came from *iubeō*, that *rīsī* came from *rīdeō* or that *vīdī* came from *videō*? And that's just to look at the 2nd conjugation. When we look at the 3rd conjugation, things get even worse. *Lūsī* from *lūdō*, *lēgī* from *legō*, *scrīpsī* from *scrībō*? I ask you! The answer is quite simply that you cannot with any degree of certainty guess how a verb will go; you just have to learn its principal parts when you meet it.

Exercise 6.14

1. Using the verbs from the list below, write out the following tenses (with meanings):
    (a) Present tense of *dīcō*.
    (b) Imperfect tense of *legō*.
    (c) Perfect tense of *scrībō*.

2. Then write out the perfect tense of any *three* other verbs from the list.

dīcō, -ere, dīxī, dictum	=	I say
dūcō, -ere, dūxī, ductum	=	I lead
legō, -ere, lēgī, lēctum	=	I read, choose
lūdō, -ere, lūsī, lūsum	=	I play
discēdō, -ere, discessī, discessum	=	I depart
scrībō, -ere, scrīpsī, scrīptum	=	I write
ostendō, -ere, ostendī, ostentum	=	I show

Exercise 6.15

Translate into English:

1. *īnsulam nautae ostendimus.*
2. *puerī et puellae librōs legēbant.*
3. *in agrō lūdunt.*
4. *quis fēminās in templum dūcit?*
5. *multī virī ex oppidō discēdunt.*
6. *Quīntus, poēta, librōs scrīpsit.*
7. *rēgīna īnsulae incolās regēbat.*
8. *suntne fēminae pulchrae?*
9. *rīdentne dominī?*
10. *dominīne puerōs laudant?*

Exercise 6.16

Translate into Latin:

1. The man is building a wall.
2. The girl is praising the teacher.
3. The poet fears the sword.
4. The farmer sees the horse.
5. The slave fears the master.
6. Why did the little boys remain in the island?
7. Do the inhabitants read books in the town?
8. The farmers were departing from the fields.

Exercise 6.17

Translate the following questions:

1. Why were you shouting?
2. Who is singing?
3. Were they preparing the wine?
4. Who prepared the food?
5. Where is the wine?
6. Did you call me, master?
7. What frightened the girl?
8. Who did not see the boy?

Exercise 6.18

Study the following passage, read it aloud, and then answer the questions that follow:

The birth of Romulus and his twin brother Remus

1 *Alba Longa in Ītaliā est; oppidum est.. Albam Longam*
  Proca rēxit. Numitor et Amūlius Procae filiī erant. post
  Procam Numitor Albam Longam rēxit. Amūlius malus
  erat. Numitōrem superāvit et ipse Albam Longam rēxit.
5 *Numitor fīliam habuit, Rhēam Silviam. Mārs, bellī deus,*
  Rhēam Silviam amāvit. Mārs et Rhēa Silvia fīliōs
  gemellōs habuērunt, Rōmulum et Remum.

Alba Longa = name of town
Proca, -ae, m. = Proca
post (+ acc.) = after
Numitōrem: this is the acc. sing. of
Numitor (a 3rd declension noun!)
ipse = he himself
gemellus, -ī, m. = twin

N.B. Note how the passage ends, not with a verb (as is more usual), but with the words *Rōmulum et Remum*. This is for emphasis. Note also how in our somewhat tiresome way, the English pronunciation of the vowels in Romulus and Remus is the exact opposite of the Latin pronunciation:

Latin		**English**
Rōmulus (long o)	=	*Rŏmulus* (short o)
Rĕmus (short e)	=	*Rēmus* (long e)

1. Answer the following questions:
   (a) In line 1, where was Alba Longa?
   (b) In lines 1- 2, who was Proca (the answer is a he, despite the *-a* ending)?
   (c) In line 4, what did Amulius do to his brother?
   (d) In line 5, who was Rhea Silvia?
   (e) In line 5, who was Mars?

2. Translate the passage into manly English.

3. Answer the following questions:
   (a) *Ītaliā* (line 1): in which case is this word? How do you know?
   (b) *rēxit* (line 2): in which tense is this verb?
   (c) *superāvit* (line 4): put this verb into the imperfect tense.
   (d) *bellī* (line 5): in which case is this word?
   (e) *Rōmulum et Remum* (line 7): in which case are these words and why?

Vocabulary 6

ōlim = once upon a time
bene = well
dīcō, dīcere, dīxī, dictum = I say
diū = for a long time
dūcō, -ere, dūxī, ductum = I lead
fortiter = bravely
iam = now, already
magnopere = greatly
auxilium, -iī, n. = help
nāvigō, -āre, -āvī, -ātum = I sail

vīnum, -ī, n. = wine
oppugnō, -āre, -āvī, -ātum = I attack*
perīculum, -ī, n. = danger
regō, -ere, rēxī, rēctum = I rule
spectō, -āre, -āvī, -ātum = I watch
timeō, -ēre, -uī = I fear
turba, -ae, f. = crowd, disturbance
unda, -ae, f. = wave
ventus, -ī, m. = wind
moneō, -ēre, -uī, -itum = I warn, advise

*****N.B.** *oppugnō* is used of attacking a place, not a person.

So here we are; unstoppable aren't we?

Chapter 7

Ordinals: 1st-10th

Remember our great mathematical excursion into the numbers I – X (1 – 10). In case you didn't know, ordinary numbers like the ones we've done are called **cardinal** numbers. I can't really explain this very satisfactorily. I don't think it's got anything to do with cardinals, though there might at some stage have been ten of these. No that won't do at all, since eleven and twelve all the way to a million or a billion or beyond as far as you can go are cardinal. And I doubt if there ever were a billion or more cardinals. Personally I always remember it by thinking of the numbers written on *cards* (the two of hearts, the three of spades etc.), but you may have your own views on this. Oh, of course! I forgot to say that the word comes from the Latin *cardinālis* which will, no doubt, clear the whole thing up: it means, well… er… "of or pertaining to a door-hinge". Sorry! It's not my fault.

The **ordinals** however make a bit more sense; they are adjectives telling us in what *order* someone or something comes; you, for example are doubtless first, but there must be some lesser beings who are second or third or even billionth.

Here are the first ten ordinal numbers. Note that, being adjectives, they have masculine, feminine and neuter endings, just like *bonus*:

prīmus, -a, -um	=	first
secundus, -a, -um	=	second
tertius, -a, -um	=	third
quārtus, -a, -um	=	fourth
quīntus, -a, -um	=	fifth
sextus, -a, -um	=	sixth
septimus, -a, -um	=	seventh
octāvus, -a, -um	=	eighth
nōnus, -a, -um	=	ninth
decimus, -a, -um	=	tenth

Exercise 7.1

Translate into English:

1. *magister quīntum librum legit.*
2. *trēs fēminae in quārtum agrum festīnābant.*
3. *magister secundum librum legēbat.*
4. *quis decimus fīlius est?*
5. *nōnusne fīlius es?*
6. *dominus septimō servō pecūniam dedit.*
7. *in octāvā viā habitābam.*
8. *ubi est sextum scūtum?*
9. *prīmus puer et tertia puella in templō erant.*
10. *quis librum poētae bonī lēgit?*

4th conjugation: audiō

And now, with much beating of drums, comes the final regular conjugation of verbs, the 4th:

---

audiō, audīre, audīvī, audītum = I hear

Present tense

1st person singular	audiō	=	I hear
2nd person singular	audīs	=	you (s.) hear
3rd person singular	audit	=	he, she or it hears
1st person plural	audīmus	=	we hear
2nd person plural	audītis	=	you (pl.) hear
3rd person plural	audiunt	=	they hear

Here we have our usual endings of -ō, -s, -t etc., added to the stem *audi/audi*, but beware! Where is the sting? You've got it. The third person plural *audiunt* teaches us to be ever on the alert and never to be lulled into a state of false security. After all, that *u* seems to be there out of mere spite. However, let's be grateful for the regularity of the rest of it.

Imperfect tense

1st person singular	audiēbam	=	I was hearing
2nd person singular	audiēbās	=	you (s.) were hearing
3rd person singular	audiēbat	=	he, she, it was hearing
1st person plural	audiēbāmus	=	we were hearing
2nd person plural	audiēbātis	=	you (pl.) were hearing
3rd person plural	audiēbant	=	they were hearing

Perfect tense

1st person singular	audīvī	=	I have heard
2nd person singular	audīvistī	=	you (s.) have heard
3rd person singular	audīvit	=	he, she it has heard
1st person plural	audīvimus	=	we have heard
2nd person plural	audīvistis	=	you (pl.) have heard
3rd person plural	audīvērunt	=	they have heard

Note that 4th conjugation verbs tend to go -iō, -īre, -īvī, -ītum. If the 2nd principal part goes -īre then you can be sure that it is 4th conjugation. Not all 4th conjugation verbs follow the -īvī, -ītum pattern, as *veniō* (below) proves.

Exercise 7.2

Write out the following tenses:

1. Present tense of *veniō, -īre, vēnī, ventum* = I come
2. Imperfect tense of *dormiō, -īre, -īvī, -ītum* = I sleep
3. Perfect tense of *veniō, -īre, vēnī, ventum* = I come

Exercise 7.3

Translate into English, in more than one way if you think it a good idea:

1. *Quīntī fīlius caelum spectābat.*
2. *timēbantne puellae perīcula?*
3. *quid dīxit prīmus puer?*
4. *cūr dominī ancillās ex templō dūxērunt?*
5. *agricola, ubi equum audīvit, in agrum vēnit.*
6. *malī nautae hastās et gladiōs legēbant.*
7. *bonus puer novum librum legēbat.*
8. *puerī et puellae in oppidō dormiunt.*
9. *equus in terrā stābat.*
10. *puellae, quod timēbant, nōn respondērunt.*

Exercise 7.4

Translate into Latin:

1. The first sailor has a spear.
2. The second teacher is carrying a book.
3. The woman fears the battle.
4. The girl is watching the island.
5. The boy sees the horse.
6. The first men were departing from the second temple.
7. What are the farmers showing to the sailors?
8. The famous teacher wrote a tenth book.
9. The beautiful woman used to live in the eighth street.
10. Was it to the seventh boy that you gave a book?

Exercise 7.5

Of what English words do the following Latin ones remind you?

1. *legō*
2. *scrībō*
3. *regō*
4. *servus*
5. *fortiter*
6. *quārtus*
7. *octāvus*
8. *decimus*

Exercise 7.6

Translate into Latin:

1. The girl fears the sailor.
2. The farmer watches the sky.
3. The teacher praises the boy.
4. The master frightens the slave.
5. The messenger hears the poet.
6. The girl fears the sailors; she therefore comes out of the temple.

7.   Were they coming from the island?
8.   Have you (pl.) heard the messengers?
9.   Who was leading the sailors into the town?
10.   Why were the inhabitants warning the maid-servants?

Exercise 7.7

And now at last comes the moment which you have all been waiting for so avidly. I congratulate you on your patience, and will reward you instantly by continuing the story which we left unfinished.

Read through the piece below carefully, and then answer the questions that follow it:

The plot thickens as the sailors approach the town and the inhabitants take action...

1   *nautae ad oppidum festīnant et cibum ibi cōnsūmere et vīnum bibere et aurum dēmere cōnstituunt, sed Mārcus, agricolae fīlius, ab agrīs discēdit et per sēcrētās viās in oppidum currit. ibi "malī nautae" clāmat "in oppidum*
5   *festīnant et aurum nostrum petunt". statim incolae, ubi dē nautīs audiunt, cibum et vīnum dēlent et aurum in locum sēcrētūm portant.*

dēmō, -ere = I take away
cōnstituō, -ere = I decide
sēcrētus, -a, um: three guesses what this means!
currō, -ere = I run
petō, -ere = I seek
statim = immediately

1.   Answer the following questions:
(a) Mention the thing that the sailors decide to do in line 1 when they reach the town.
(b) Mention another thing from line 2.
(c) Mention yet another from line 2.
(d) In lines 2-5, who warns the inhabitants about the sailors?
(e) In lines 3-4, how does he get through to the town?
(f) In lines 5-7, mention three things that the inhabitants do on hearing the boy.
(g) In line 5, which word tells us that the inhabitants waste no time?

2.   Translate the passage into clever English.

3.   Answer the following questions:
(a) In line 2 what part of *bibō* is *bibere?*
(b) In line 2 what part of *dēmō* is *dēmere?*
(c) In line 2 what do we learn about the conjugation of *bibō* from *bibere?*
(d) In line 3 what case is *agricolae?*
(e) In this piece find and translate two examples of a preposition followed by the accusative.
(f) In this piece find and translate two examples of a preposition followed by the ablative.
(g) Put *dēlent* in line 6 into the perfect tense.
(h) In line 7 which Latin word is the object of *portant?*

Vēnī, vīdī, vīcī!

vēnī, vīdī, vīcī!

Now for some much needed **revision** of our wonderful verbs with crazy principal parts. We have met the four main conjugations and are only too familiar with the fact that many, many verbs have principal parts that cannot be predicted and just have to be learnt. One consolation can be gleaned from this sorry tale, however, namely that you now know how Julius Caesar could come out with his famous crack (illustrating his endearing modesty) after having defeated some unfortunate people* (one of his favourite pastimes): **vēnī, vīdī, vīcī,** meaning "I came, I saw, I conquered". You'll have to take *vīcī* (from *vincō*) on trust for the moment, but I assure you that that's what it means.

*In case you thought we didn't know, he had conquered Pharnaces II at Zela. Apologies for the name-dropping!

So here we go with a host of funny principal parts (many of which you have met already):

1st conjugation

dō	*dăre*	*dedī*	*dătum*	=	I give
stō	*stāre*	*stetī*	*stătum*	=	I stand

2nd conjugation

iubeō	*iubēre*	*iussī*	*iussum*	=	I order
maneō	*manēre*	*mānsī*	*mānsum*	=	I remain
moveō	*movēre*	*mōvī*	*mōtum*	=	I move (transitive)
respondeō	*respondēre*	*respondī*	*respōnsum*	=	I reply
rīdeō	*rīdēre*	*rīsī*	*rīsum*	=	I laugh
videō	*vidēre*	*vīdī*	*vīsum*	=	I see
dēleo	*dēlēre*	*dēlēvī*	*dēlētum*	=	I destroy

3rd conjugation

cōnsūmō	*cōnsūmere*	*cōnsūmpsī*	*cōnsūmptum*	=	I eat
discēdō	*discēdere*	*discessī*	*discessum*	=	I depart
lūdō	*lūdere*	*lūsī*	*lūsum*	=	I play
mittō	*mittere*	*mīsī*	*missum*	=	I send
scrībō	*scrībere*	*scrīpsī*	*scrīptum*	=	I write
bibō	*bibere*	*bibī*	-	=	I drink
currō	*currere*	*cucurrī*	*cursum*	=	I run
pōnō	*pōnere*	*posuī*	*positum*	=	I put, place
cōnstituō	*cōnstituere*	*cōnstituī*	*cōnstitūtum*	=	I decide

4th conjugation

veniō	*venīre*	*vēnī*	*ventum*	=	I come

One of these, *cōnstituō*, as you will immediately see, has a stem (the bit before the *ō* of the 1st person singular) which doesn't end in a consonant (like the other 3rd conjugation verbs), but in a *u*. There are a number of 3rd conjugation verbs in *-uō*. The main thing to note about such verbs is the rather odd-looking clash of vowels in the present tense. For example *cōnstituō* goes *cōnstituō, cōnstituis, cōnstituit, cōnstituimus, cōnstituitis, cōnstituunt* (note the funny-looking double *u*).

Another one to look out for is *currō*; just look at that perfect tense: *cucurrī*. It sounds like something you do in the kitchen, or as if it had gone cuckoo (pun intended – sorry)! Nor is it alone in behaving like this. And needless to say, there is a nice long name for this weird behaviour: reduplication. The first syllable of the verb *currō* is reduplicated (i.e. repeated) in forming the perfect tense. Look out for similar verbs, now that you know this long word.

And while we are at it, take a look at *pōnō*, behaving in the last two principal parts as if it were a 2nd conjugation verb (all that *-uī, -itum* stuff). Well really!

Exercise 7.8

Translate into English:

1. *duo puerī in viā lūsērunt.*
2. *poēta trēs librōs scrīpsit.*
3. *cūr ex oppidō cucurristī?*
4. *dominus in templum servōs dūxit.*
5. *rēgīna diū rēxit.*
6. *cōnsūmpsistīne cibum?*
7. *nūntium in oppidum mīsī.*
8. *agricola ex agrō discessit.*

Exercise 7.9

Translate into Latin:

1. The girl is warning the slave.
2. The master is calling the maid-servant.
3. The woman praises the poet.
4. The boy watches the field.
5. The messengers have departed from the island.
6. What have the poets said to the inhabitants?
7. The farmers led four horses into the field.
8. The boys have played in the town.

Exercise 7.10

And now for some revision of vocabulary. What is the Latin for the following. Remember to give full details (nominative singular, genitive singular, gender and meaning) as in the example:

E.g. *nauta, nautae*, m. = sailor

1. A farmer
2. A woman
3. The inhabitant
4. A field
5. A teacher
6. War
7. An island
8. Wine
9. A wall
10. The battle
11. A horse
12. Anger

Exercise 7.11

We now return to the harrowing tale of Romulus and Remus...

Read the passage, and answer the questions that follow:

Romulus and Remus are thrown into the River Tiber and have an unusual upbringing.

1   *Amūlius, quod Rhēa Silvia fīliōs habuit, magnopere īrātus erat; <u>gemellōs</u> igitur in <u>fluvium</u> <u>iacere</u> servōs iussit; fluvius Tiberis erat. ibi parvōs <u>gemellōs</u> <u>lupa</u> <u>servāvit</u> et <u>nūtrīcāvit</u>. <u>posteā</u> <u>pāstor</u>, Faustulus, ad <u>marītam</u> portāvit;*
5   *<u>gemellōs</u> <u>cūrābant</u>. tandem Rōmulus et Remus magnī et validī erant et multōs amīcōs habuērunt. Albam Longam intrāvērunt et ibi dīxērunt "fīliī sumus <u>Mārtis</u> et Rhēae Silviae; Rōmulus et Remus sumus."*

gemellus, -ī, m. = twin
fluvius, -iī, m. = river
iacere = to throw
lupa, -ae, f. = she-wolf
servō, -āre = I save
nūtrīcō, -āre = I feed, suckle
posteā = afterwards
pāstor = a shepherd (3rd. dec.)
marīta, -ae, f. = wife
cūrō, -āre = I care for
Mārtis : gen. sing. of Mārs (3rd dec.)

1.   Answer the following questions:
   (a) In lines 1-2, what did Amulius feel about Rhea Silvia's sons?
   (b) In line 2, how did he deal with them?
   (c) In lines 3-4, who brought the twins up? Answer in full.
   (d) In lines 5-6, how are Romulus and Remus described when they are grown up?
   (e) In line 6, what else do we learn about them?

2.	Translate the passage into harrowing English.

3.	Answer the following questions:
	(a) *habuit* (line 1): give the principal parts of the verb from which this comes.
	(b) *iussit* (line 2): give the principal parts of the verb from which this comes.
	(c) Write down and translate a noun from the passage with an adjective in agreement.
	(d) *dīxērunt* (line 7): give the principal parts of this verb.
	(e) *sumus* (line 7): Put *sumus* into the imperfect tense.

Vocabulary 7

prīmus, -a, -um = first
secundus, -a, -um = second
tertius, -a, -um = third
quārtus, -a, -um = fourth
quīntus, -a, -um = fifth
sextus, -a. -um = sixth
septimus, -a, -um = seventh
octāvus, -a, -um = eighth
nōnus, -a, -um = ninth
decimus, -a, -um = tenth

audiō, -īre, -īvī, -ītum = I hear, listen to
deinde = next, then
dormiō, -īre, -īvī, -ītum = I sleep
ibi = there
*igitur** = therefore
itaque = therefore, and so
iterum = again
mox = soon
quod = because
veniō, -īre, vēnī, ventum = I come

***N.B.** This word is not generally written as the 1st word in a clause.

E.g.	*Amūlius igitur gemellōs timuit* = Therefore Amulius feared the twins.

We are beginning to get dangerously near the end...

Chapter 8

Mixed conjugation

Back to verbs; and we've really got something rather special coming. Remember platform 9¾ in *Harry Potter*? Well, we've got something pretty well like it in Latin grammar, namely conjugation 3½, sometimes called the mixed conjugation. The unexpected thing about mixed conjugation verbs is that although they end in *-iō* they behave more like 3rd conjugation verbs than 4th. Three verbs which belong to this conjugation are immensely frequent and – best of all – they all go in exactly the same way (until further notice). Let us take *capio* = I take or capture as our model.

---

capiō = I take, capture

Present tense

1st person singular	*capiō*	=	I take
2nd person singular	*capis*	=	you (s.) take
3rd person singular	*capit*	=	he, she, it takes
1st person plural	*capimus*	=	we take
2nd person plural	*capitis*	=	you (pl.) take
3rd person plural	*capiunt*	=	they take

Imperfect tense

1st person singular	*capiēbam*	=	I was taking
2nd person singular	*capiēbās*	=	you (s.) were taking
3rd person singular	*capiēbat*	=	he, she, it was taking
1st person plural	*capiēbāmus*	=	we were taking
2nd person plural	*capiēbātis*	=	you (pl.) were taking
3rd person plural	*capiēbant*	=	they were taking

Perfect tense

1st person singular	*cēpī*	=	I have taken
2nd person singular	*cēpistī*	=	you (s.) have taken
3rd person singular	*cēpit*	=	he, she, it has taken
1st person plural	*cēpimus*	=	we have taken
2nd person plural	*cēpistis*	=	you (pl.) have taken
3rd person plural	*cēpērunt*	=	they have taken

Points to note

1. The 1st principal part of a mixed conjugation verb ends in *-iō* (as in *audiō*).
2. The 2nd principal part of a mixed conjugation verb ends in *-ere* (as in *regō*).
3. The vowels in the present tense endings are short (as in *regō*).
4. The 3rd person plural of the present tense goes *-iunt* (as in *audiō*).

See why they call it mixed?

Like *capio* go *faciō* = "I do" or "I make" and *iaciō* = "I throw", which might not seem quite as frequent as *capiō* and *faciō,* but in fact the Romans spent at least half their time throwing things at people. Remember Julius Caesar? Another verb, *cupiō,* is similar to *capiō,* in its present and imperfect tenses. We shall soon see, however, that not only is it mixed, but it is hopelessly mixed up. Still, for the moment let us accept it gratefully, since it means I desire, wish, or want and we have longed for a verb with this meaning for ages.

Exercise 8.1

Translate into English:

1. *servī, ubi mūrum faciunt, cantant.*
2. *quid nautae ex oppidō cēpērunt?*
3. *nautae sagittās in oppidum iacere cupiunt.*
4. *ventus multās undās fēcit.*
5. *hastās in mūrum iaciēbāmus.*
6. *cupitisne librum legere?*
7. *cūr cibum in oppidō parāre nōn cupis?*
8. *aurum et pecūniam capere cupiō.*

Exercise 8.2

Translate into Latin:

1. The woman is preparing food.
2. The boy praises the poet.
3. The teacher's son sees the field.
4. The sailor is carrying a sword.
5. What were they taking from the island?
6. We were throwing shields into high places.
7. What are messengers doing in the temple?
8. The little girls wished to run through the fields.

And now your patience is about to be rewarded. For here comes the continuation of one of our stories, bringing it to a happy ending.

Exercise 8.3

Read the piece below carefully, remembering to savour the sounds of the glorious Latin, and then answer the questions that follow it.

The wicked sailors are foiled and the inhabitants rejoice.

1　*nautae, ubi prope oppidum sunt, cōnsūmere et bibere*
　magnopere cupiunt. mox in oppidum currunt; ibi tamen
　cibus nōn est, vīnum nōn est. incolās vocant: etiam
　incolae ibi nōn sunt. aurum ex terrā capere cupiunt:
5　*terram movent: aurum ibi nōn est. tandem nautae,*
　miserī et īrātī, ex oppidō et ex īnsulā discēdere
　cōnstituunt. incolae spectant et rīdent et "quod tūtī
　sumus," cantant, "laetī sumus".

1.　Answer the following:
　(a) In line 1, where are the sailors?
　(b) In lines 1-2, what were the sailors thinking about most?
　(c) In line 2, to what does *ibi* refer?
　(d) In line 4, did the sailors find the inhabitants in the town?
　(e) *terram movent* (line 5), to what activity do you think these two words refer?
　(f) In line 6, why were the sailors *miserī* ?
　(g) In line 6, why were they *īrātī*?
　(h) In lines 6-7, what did the sailors finally do?
　(i) In line 7, we have the word *rīdent*. Why did the inhabitants do this?

2. Now translate the piece into triumphant English, and sigh with relief that all was well.

3. Answer the following:
   (a) In line 1, what does *ubi* mean when followed by a question mark?
   (b) In line 1, what parts of the verbs are *cōnsūmere* and *bibere?*
   (c) Give any other examples of this part in this piece, and translate them.
   (d) In line 3, in what case is *incolās*? And what is it governed by?
   (e) In line 4, in what case is *aurum?*
   (f) In line 5, in what case is *aurum?*
   (g) In line 6, in what case are *miserī* and *īrātī* and with what noun do they agree?

Exercise 8.4

Translate into English:

1. *Quīntus incolās dē perīculō monuit.*
2. *fēminae multum aurum habuērunt.*
3. *tenuistīne gladium et hastam?*
4. *puerī, ubi magister vēnit, dormiēbant.*
5. *Aulus equum nōn timuit.*
6. *cūr equōs terruistis?*
7. *quid dē agricolīs audiēbātis?*
8. *magistrī cum puerīs in templum veniēbant.*
9. *verba poētae audiēbāmus.*
10. *verba poētae audīvimus.*

Exercise 8.5

Translate into Latin:

1. The master frightens the slave.
2. The girl fears the master.
3. The savage sailor is holding a spear.
4. The maid-servant is preparing food.
5. The boy is carrying a shield.
6. The farmers warned the inhabitants about the sailors.
7. The girls used to hear the poets.
8. When the boys came, they heard the master.
9. The horses were sleeping in the field.
10. The inhabitants had much gold.

Imperatives

Some more about verbs; never ending I fear (or nearly so). So here's a new part altogether, though it's rather a nasty bossy one, I'm afraid. It's called the imperative, and it's all to do with ordering people about, something which the Romans were very good at doing. There is no first person imperative. The third person of the imperative exists but is rare enough for us to forget it for quite a long time. It's the second persons (singular and plural) which really matter. After all, one nearly always issues orders (if one issues them at all) to the person to whom one is talking, i.e. you!

The 2nd person singular of the imperative can be formed from the present infinitive by dropping its final '*-re*'. Take '*amāre*' for example, drop the '*-re*' and hey-presto there you are with the imperative '*amā*' meaning 'love'!

Singular

1st conjugation	*amā*	=	love!
2nd conjugation	*monē*	=	warn, advise!
3rd conjugation	*rege*	=	rule!
4th conjugation	*audī*	=	hear!
3½ conjugation	*cape*	=	take!

N.B. The imperative of *dō* (present infinitive *dăre*, with a short *ă*) is *dā* (with a long *ā*).

Plural

All these imperatives have a 2nd person plural form too. This really is nice and easy, without any irregulars. Once again we do a sort of conjuring trick. Take the 2nd person plural of the present tense, remove the '*-tis*' and replace it with '*-te*' and once again, hey-presto: you've got it.

1st conjugation	*amāte*	=	love!
2nd conjugation	*monēte*	=	warn!
3rd conjugation	*regite*	=	rule!
4th conjugation	*audīte*	=	hear!
3½ conjugation	*capite*	=	take!

N.B. The plural imperative of *dō* is *dăte* with a short *ă* (which just proves that the rule always works; 2nd person plural of *dō* = *dătis*).

And while we are talking about the length of vowels, note (out of interest) that *věnī* (= come!) is the imperative, while *vēnī* (= I have come) is the perfect. See the importance of quantities, eh?

Irregular imperatives

Needless to say, there are some famous irregular 2nd person singular imperatives, most of them from verbs we have learnt. For example:

dīcō	goes	*dīc*
dūcō	goes	*dūc*
faciō	goes	*fac*

With these verbs it is almost as if they had run out of ink (or its equivalent) before they could reach the final '*e*'. Perhaps you've noticed that '*e*' does seem to come in for rather a bad time. Remember nouns like *magister* which drop their '*e*'? And adjectives like *pulcher?* Poor old '*e*'.

More about sum

Remember how totally irregular *sum* is? Here are two or three points to note.

1. It has its own type of present infinitive which is slightly odd to look at, namely *esse*.
2. In the 2nd person imperative, *sum* goes *es* (singular) and *este* (plural).
3. It has no supine.

Exercise 8.6

Translate into English:

1. *verba magistrī audī!*
2. *tres mūrōs in agrō aedificā!*
3. *amīce, quattuor librōs in oppidum cape!*
4. *parvōs puerōs in templum dūc!*
5. *serve, in oppidō manē!*
6. *magistrī, ab agrīs discēdite!*
7. *puerī, in oppidum venīte!*
8. *agricolās dē nautīs monēte!*
9. *puellae, fēminīs respondēte!*
10. *ancillae, cibum parāte!*

Exercise 8.7

Translate into Latin.

1. The master advises the boys.
2. The sailor is holding a sword.
3. The girl is watching the poet.
4. The boy calls the maid-servant.
5. Marcus, lead the horses into the field.
6. Boys, take the books into the temple.
7. Depart from the beautiful island, Aulus.
8. Walk in the field with the little girls Sextus.
9. Cassia, eat your food near the town.
10. Farmers, order the savage men to run out of the fields.

Exercise 8.8

Read the following passage aloud and answer the questions that follow:

Romulus and Remus found Rome but alas, the story ends sadly

1 *Amūlius Rōmulum et Remum, ubi Albam Longam intrāvērunt, magnopere timuit; Amūlium Rōmulus et Remus necāvērunt. Numitor iterum Albam Longam rēxit; <u>gemellī</u> novum oppidum <u>condere</u> cōnstituērunt; oppidum*	*gemellus, -ī*, m. = twin
5 *Rōma erat. Rōmulus mūrōs aedificāvit et laetus spectābat; Remus tamen mūrōs <u>trānsiluit</u>; Rōmulus, quod Remus mūrōs Rōmae <u>trānsiluit</u>, Remum īrātus necāvit.*	*condō, -ere* = I found, establish *trānsilio, -īre, -uī* = I jump over

1. Answer the following:
   (a) In lines 1-2, what were Amulius' feelings on the twins' arrival?
   (b) In lines 2-3, what fact shows how his feelings were justified?
   (c) In line 4, what did the twins decide to do?
   (d) In lines 5-6, what was Romulus doing after he had built the walls of Rome?
   (e) In line 5, how did he feel while he was doing this?
   (f) In line 6 what did Remus do?
   (g) In lines 6-7, how did this make Romulus feel and what did he do?

2. Translate the passage into bloodthirsty English.

3. Answer the following:
   (a) *timuit* (line 2): give the principal parts of this verb.
   (b) *rēxit* (line 3): give the principal parts of this verb.
   (c) *oppidum* (line 4): in which case is this noun the first time it appears in the line?
   (d) *oppidum* (line 4): in which case is this noun the second time it appears in the line?
   (e) *īrātus* (line 7): with which noun does this agree?

Revision of prepositions

A brief word about the presentation of prepositions. Remember that a preposition should always be learnt together with the case that follows it and its meaning.

E.g. *ā* or *ab* + abl.   =   from, by
in + acc.   =   into, on to
in + abl.   =   in, on

Exercise 8.9

Give the Latin for the following, as in the example.

E.g. with = *cum* + abl.

1.	near	5.	out of
2.	against	6.	across
3.	to	7.	through
4.	into	8.	in

Exercise 8.10

Of what English words do the following Latin words remind us?

(a) *prīmus*
(b) *multus*
(c) *clārus*
(d) *altus*
(e) *perīculum* (This one needs a bit of squashing.)

Adsum and absum

And now for a cluster of words round our old friend *sum.* You may have heard the little ditty:

Caesar adsum jam* forte, Pompey aderat.

(*See our words in the introduction on the old-fashioned use of *j* on page 6.)

You may also know that in some schools a pupil is required to say *adsum* = "I am present" when his name is read out in roll-call. No? Well anyway, *absum* and *adsum* are good examples of Latin **compound verbs:**

1. *absum* is made up of *ab/ā* + *sum* = "to be from", and thus "to be absent";
2. *adsum* is made up of *ad* + *sum* = "to be to", and thus "to be present".

The *sum* part of these two verbs is easy and goes just like *sum* itself:

---

absum, abesse, āfuī = I am absent

Present tense

1st person singular	absum	I am absent
2nd person singular	abes	you (s.) are absent
3rd person singular	abest	he, she, it, is absent
1st person plural	absumus	we are absent
2nd person plural	abestis	you (pl.) are absent
3rd person plural	absunt	they are absent

Imperfect tense

1st person singular	aberam	I was absent
2nd person singular	aberās	you (s.) were absent
3rd person singular	aberat	he, she, it, was absent
1st person plural	aberāmus	we were absent
2nd person plural	aberātis	you (pl.) were absent
3rd person plural	aberant	they were absent

Perfect tense

1st person singular	āfuī	I have been absent
2nd person singular	āfuistī	you (s.) have been absent
3rd person singular	āfuit	he, she, it, has been absent
1st person plural	āfuimus	we have been absent
2nd person plural	āfuistis	you (pl.) have been absent
3rd person plural	āfuērunt	they have been absent

Adsum, adesse, adfuī works in exactly the same way:

Present:	adsum	=	I am present
Imperfect	aderam	=	I was present
Perfect	adfuī	=	I have been present

The imperatives of *adsum,* which are *ades* and *adeste,* from the meaning 'be present!' very often come to mean "come here!"; *adeste* is famously found in the carol "*adeste, fidēlēs!*" ("O come, all ye faithful!").

Exercise 8.11

Translate into English:

1. *puerī ā templō aberant.*
2. *agricolae saepe ab agrīs absunt.*
3. *semper ā proeliō abesse cupimus.*
4. *cūr ab oppidō āfuistī?*
5. *nūntiī ā locō āfuērunt.*
6. *bonae fēminae ad* templum adesse cōnstituērunt.*
7. *quis ibi iam adest?*
8. *nautae fīlia ad* viam aderat.*
9. *itaque ad* mūrum adfuimus.*
10. *serve, ad mē ades.*

*Note that *ad* + accusative often means 'at'.

Exercise 8.12

Translate into Latin:

1. Aulus is building a wall
2. The maid-servant prepares food.
3. The sailor holds a shield.
4. Marcus enters the field.
5. The poet carries a book.
6. We are absent from the town.
7. Because the boys were not present, they were absent. (Brilliant logic.)
8. The maid-servants are never absent from the island.
9. The allies have been present.
10. Good girls are always present.

And here comes a completely new story to end this chapter with. And Chapter 9 is going to be more exciting still. Oh! how lucky you are!

Exercise 8.13

Read the piece below carefully, and then answer the questions that follow it:

An adventure by sea

1 *ōlim, quīnque puerī cum quīnque puellīs novam īnsulam* <u>*petere*</u> *cōnstituērunt. ibi nōn incolās superāre cupiēbant sed invenīre aurum. gladiōs et hastās trāns undās nōn cēpērunt, sed multum cibum et multam aquam et*

petō, -ere = I seek

5 *magnum librum. librum scrīpsit poēta Quīntus et parvīs nautīs dedit; pulcher erat et pulchra verba* <u>*continuit*</u>*; nautae librum magnopere amābant. fortiter per undās nāvigābant; ubi ventī bonī fuērunt, laetī erant; sed ubi malī fuērunt, quod in magnō perīculō erant, miserī erant.*

contineō, -ēre = I contain

10 *tandem īnsulam invēnērunt; in oppidum festīnant. ibi incolae nautīs "*<u>*salvēte!*</u>*" dīcunt.*

salvēte = greetings! welcome!

*N.B. *inveniō* is a compound of *veniō* = 'I come upon', hence 'I find'. (Inventive, eh?)

1.	Answer the following:
	(a) In line 1, when did all this happen?
	(b) In line 1, which word tells us this?
	(c) In lines 2-4, why do you think the sailors did not take *gladiī* or *hastae?*
	(d) In line 4, what did they take which one would have expected them to take?
	(e) In line 5, what unexpected thing did they take?
	(f) In lines 5-6, who gave them this thing?
	(g) In line 6, what were inside this thing?
	(h) In lines 8-9, was the journey an easy one? Explain your answer.

2.	Translate this passage nautically, and see if you can guess what is going to happen.

3.	Answer the following:
	(a) In line 2, what part of *petō* is *petere?*
	(b) Are there any other examples of this part in the piece?
	(c) In line 2, what conjugation is *cōnstituērunt?*
	(d) In line 6, what is the subject of *pulcher erat?*
	(e) In line 6, in what case are the words *pulchra verba?*
	(f) In line 7, which word describes the sailors' state of mind while sailing?
	(g) In line 8 we are told that the sailors were happy when the winds were good. What change
		would be necessary to the words *ventī bonī fuērunt* if we were to say "**the wind was good**"?
	(h) In line 9, which Latin words state the reason why the sailors were on occasions *miserī?*

Vocabulary 8

absum, abesse, āfuī (irreg.) = I am absent
adsum, adesse, adfuī (irreg.) = I am present
aurum, -ī, n. = gold
caelum, -ī, n. = sky
clārus, -a, -um = famous, clear, bright
gladius, gladiī, m. = sword
iubeō, -ēre, iussī, iussum = I order
nōtus, -a, -um = well-known
novus, -a, -um = new
nūntius, nūntiī, m. = messenger, message

perterritus, -a, -um = terrified
proelium, -iī, n. = battle
saepe = often
saevus, -a, -um = savage
scūtum, -ī, n. = shield
semper = always
socius, -iī, m. = ally
statim = immediately
tūtus, -a, -um = safe
validus, -a, -um = strong

Alas! Only two more chapters; but what chapters!

Chapter 9

Subordinate clauses

Much fuss can be made about these little creatures, and in later books much fuss will be made by us too! But for now, all you need to know is that a sentence can be made up of a number of clauses, and that a clause must contain a verb. Sometimes the clauses in a sentence are joined by a conjunction such as *et* = and, *sed* = but, *quod* = because or *ubi* = when.

E.g.   *puella cantat* **et** *puer clāmat* = the girl is singing and the boy is shouting.

Sometimes, however, we find things called subordinate clauses, which are bits of the sentence (containing a verb) which are subordinate to the main clause. Here are two examples, shown in bold:

> The boy shouts **because the girl is singing**.
> The boy shouts **when the girl sings**.

If you read the parts in bold you will quickly see that they could not stand on their own; they *need* the main bit of the sentence (in each case "The boy shouts") to make sense. This is why they are called subordinate.

Subordinate clauses can be given grand names depending on what sort of job they are doing in the sentence; the first of our examples is a causal clause, because it tells us the *cause* of the boy's shouting. The second example is a temporal clause, because it tells us *when* the boy shouts (*tempus* (3rd dec., neuter) in Latin means time).

The final thing to learn is that in Latin, a **subordinate clause** is generally (but not always) tucked *inside* the **main clause**:

E.g.   *puer,* **quod puella cantat,** *clāmat.*
       puer, **ubi puella cantat,** *clāmat.*

None of this should cause you any bother; indeed for pages and pages now you have been coping happily with subordinate clauses without even realising it. But it's nice to know, isn't it?

Exercise 9.1

Practice with subordinate clauses (more colouring!).

Copy the following sentences. Underline the main clause in green and the subordinate clause in blue. Then translate.

1.   *Rōmulus, ubi Remus mūrōs spectāvit, īrātus erat.*
2.   *Rōmulus, quod Remus mūrōs spectāvit, īrātus erat.*
3.   *Amūlius Rōmulum, ubi Albam Longam intrāvit, magnopere timuit.*
4.   *nautae, ubi prope oppidum stant, vīnum bibere cupiunt.*
5.   *Amūlius, quod Rhēa Silvia fīliōs habuit, īrātus erat.*

I think these sentence are rather fine. I hope you agree.

Exercise 9.2

Read the piece below aloud, relishing its great beauty, and then answer the questions on it:

Hannibal crosses the Alps

1 *Hannibal <u>Poenus</u> erat; ubi puer fuit, saepe iterum et iterum
   audiēbat "Rōmānī malī sunt; nōs et oppidum nostrum
   dēlēre cupiunt." in <u>Hispāniā</u> per multōs annōs erat et, ubi
   vir fuit, saepe dīcēbat "ego Rōmam dēlēre cupiō." itaque*
5 *trāns locōs altōs <u>Alpīnōs</u> in Ītaliam discēdere cōnstituit.
   multōs igitur Poenōs et multōs sociōs dūxit et discessit.
   etiam, quod Rōmānōs terrēre cupiēbat, multōs <u>elephantōs</u>
   dūxit. Hannibal Rōmānōs nōn amābat!*

Poenus = Carthaginian (pretty obvious, eh?)

Hispānia, -ae, f. = Spain

Alpīnus, -a, -um = Alpine

elephantus = this one is harder, but we will leave you to guess it.

1.   Answer the following:
     (a) In lines 1-3, what turned Hannibal against the Romans?
     (b) In line 1, how old was Hannibal when this happened?
     (c) In lines 3-4, when did he feel like doing something about it?
     (d) In line 5, what did he decide to do?
     (e) In line 6, whom did he take with him?
     (f) In lines 7-8, what else did he take, and why?
     (g) In line 8, does the final sentence of the passage add anything important to the story?
          Explain your answer.

2.   Translate the passage into Alpine-flavoured prose.

3.   Answer the following:
     (a) *Poenus* (line 1): in which case is this word?
     (b) *ubi puer fuit* (line 1): what type of clause is this?
     (c) *malī* (line 2): in which case is this word?
     (d) *cupiunt* (line 3): give the present infinitive of this verb.
     (e) *vir* (line 4): in which case is this word?
     (f) *discēdere* (line 5): what part of which verb is this?
     (g) *quod Rōmānōs terrēre cupiēbat* (line 7): what type of clause is this? Comment on its
          position in the sentence.

Exercise 9.3

Revision of verbs. Translate the following into English, making sure you get the tense right!

1. *superābat*
2. *terruit*
3. *faciēbāmus*
4. *monuērunt*
5. *rogāvit*
6. *cēpistis*
7. *dormīvistī*
8. *veniunt*
9. *mānsit*
10. *cucurrimus*

Exercise 9.4

Revision of nouns. Translate the following into Latin, making sure you get the case right!

1. Near the queen
2. In a field
3. With a boy
4. Concerning a battle
5. Out of the town
6. Into an island
7. From the temple
8. Down from the walls
9. Along a road
10. Across the waves

Exercise 9.5

Read the piece below carefully, and answer the questions on it.

A sea-adventure (continued)

1 *nautae, ubi cibum cōnsūmpsērunt et aquam bibērunt, librum in <u>mēnsā</u> posuērunt et legere cōnstituērunt. 'quid facitis?' rogāvērunt incolae. 'librum legimus' respondērunt nautae, 'quid est liber?' rogavērunt iterum. nautae nōn*
5 *respondērunt. 'quid est in librō?' 'in librō verba sunt'. nautae incolīs verba ostendērunt; incolae tamen nōn <u>comprehendērunt</u>. subitō nautae cantāvērunt. iam laetī incolae cum nautīs cantābant. dīxērunt 'etiam nōs legere cupimus; <u>docēte</u> nōs'.*

mēnsa, -ae, f. = table

comprehendō, -ere, -hendī, -hēnsum = I understand
doceō, -ēre, -uī, doctum = I teach

1. Answer the following questions:
   (a) In line 2, what did the sailors do after eating and drinking?
   (b) In lines 2-3, what did the inhabitants then do?
   (c) In line 4, of what were the inhabitants rather surprisingly ignorant?
   (d) In line 6, how did the sailors try to show the inhabitants what this thing was?
   (e) In lines 6-7, why didn't this work?
   (f) In line 7, what good idea did the sailors suddenly have?
   (g) In line 7, what Latin word shows how successful this was with the inhabitants?
   (h) In lines 8-9, what did the inhabitants now want to do?
   (i) In line 9, and how did they hope to achieve this?

2. Translate the piece happily.

3. Answer the following questions:
   (a) In line 2, from what verb does *posuērunt* come?
   (b) In line 2, what part of its verb is *legere*?
   (c) In line 5, in what case is *verba*?
   (d) In line 6, in what case is *verba*?

(e) In line 6, in what case is *incolīs?*
(f) In line 8, what is the case of *nautīs?*
(g) In line 8, why is *nautīs* in this case?
(h) In line 8, in what case is *nōs?* And in line 9?
(i) In line 9, what part of its verb is *docēte?*

Exercise 9.6

Revision of adjectives. Translate the following into Latin, making sure you make the adjective agree with the noun it describes!

1. Of the happy poets.
2. The miserable boys (nom.)
3. For the tired women.
4. With many girls.
5. O happy master!

6. Out of a big town.
7. Across deep waves.
8. Through beautiful fields.
9. A savage battle (nom.)
10. A savage battle (acc.)

Exercise 9.7

And now for something slightly different!

Across
1. Number one! (3)
3. A dog asks why. (3)
5. More than a mere lady. (3)
6. I'm very romantic now. (3, 2)
9. No I'm not. (3)
10. And now I'm back to front. (3)
11. She's yours. (3)

Down
1. Here I am again (see 1 across)! (3)
2. O sir! (1, 6)
3. What lovely sounds come forth from them! (7)
4. Get through this one backwards. (3)
7. We can just get beyond one. (3)
8. She's mine. (3)

Exercise 9.8

Read the passage below carefully, and answer the questions on it:

A sea-adventure (concluded)

1 *nautae in oppidō dormiēbant et diū ibi manēbant; incolās legere docuērunt; sed tandem in patriam nāvigāre cupiēbant. ab incolīs tamen discēdere nōn cupiēbant. et nautae et incolae miserī erant; sed tandem discēdēbant*

5 *nautae et incolīs dīxērunt "nōn aurum invēnimus sed amīcōs. laetī igitur sumus." et incolae dīxērunt "venīte iterum ad vestrōs novōs amīcōs; etiam vōs nostrī amīcī estis." et nautae, ubi iam nāvigant, "valēte" clāmant et "valēte" clāmant incolae.*

doceō, -ēre, -uī, doctum = I teach
et...et = both... and

invenio, -īre, invēnī, inventum = I find

valēte = farewell

1. Answer the following:
   (a) In lines 1-2, what did the sailors do for the inhabitants ?
   (b) In lines 2-3, how were the sailors torn in two directions (not literally I'm glad to say)?
   (c) In line 4, why were the inhabitants also unhappy?
   (d) In lines 5-6, did the sailors think their voyage had been worthwhile?
   (e) In line 6, or were they disappointed?
   (f) In lines 6-7, what did the inhabitants want the sailors to do?
   (g) In lines 6-7, can you translate *venīte iterum* by one English word?

2. Translate this concluding piece into poignant (you may have to look this word up) English.

3. Answer the following questions.
   (a) In line 2, what part of the verb is *nāvigāre?*
   (b) Does this part occur anywhere else in this piece? If so, say where.
   (c) Mention all examples of a preposition followed by its case in this piece, and say what they mean.
   (d) In line 5, what is the case of *aurum?*
   (e) Can you find two words in this piece which should not be written as the first words in their sentence. If you have found them, translate them. (If not, don't – this is very important indeed.)
   (f) Can you find and translate a 4th conjugation imperative in this piece?
   (g) In lines 5-6, what do you think is brought out by the word order of *"nōn..........amīcōs"?*

Adverbs

We deal with three types of adverb in this book. They all tell us something about the verb that they describe:

1.   Adverbs of place

These tell us *where* the verb is happening.

E.g.   **hīc** habitant = they live **here**.

2.   Adverbs of time

These tell us *when* the verb is happening.

E.g.   **subitō** discessērunt = they departed **suddenly**.

3.   Adverbs of manner

These tell us *how* the verb is happening.

E.g.   patriam **magnopere** amāmus = we love our country **greatly**.
E.g.   puerī **fortiter** pugnābant = the boys were fighting **bravely**.

Exercise 9.9

Translate the following into Latin:

1.   Who lives here?
2.   Why have you come, Aulus?
3.   The farmer's slave suddenly ran into the temple.
4.   Do the boys hear the master?
5.   Were the sailors fighting bravely?
6.   Was the beautiful book in the temple?
7.   Why did they immediately enter the town?
8.   What is she reading?
9.   Where is the queen of the island?
10. The Romans love their fatherland greatly.

Vocabulary 9

bibō, -ere, bibī = I drink
capiō, -ere, cēpī, captum = I take, capture
cōnstituō, -ere, cōnstituī, cōnstitūtum =
    I decide
cupiō, -ere, -īvī, -ītum = I want, wish, desire
currō, -ere, cucurrī, cursum = I run
dēleō, dēlēre, dēlēvī, dēlētum = I destroy
discēdō, -ere, discessī, discessum =
    I depart
faciō, -ere, fēcī, factum = I do, make
habeō, -ēre, -uī, -itum = I have

iaciō, -ere, iēci, iactum = I throw
meus, -a, -um = my
mittō, -ere, mīsī, missum = I send
noster, nostra, nostrum = our
quid? = what?
scrībō, -ere, scrīpsī, scrīptum = I write
sīc = thus
subitō = suddenly
suus, sua, suum = his (own), her (own),
    its (own) or their (own)
tuus, -a, -um = your (belonging to you (sing.))

N.B. The principal parts of *cupiō* are very odd (I warned you of this); the perfect and supine look alarmingly like a regular 4th conjugation verb, yet *cupiō* is of course mixed conjugation (3½).

It is very easy to mix up the spelling of the perfect and supine of *mittō*. You should say *mīsī* (one *s*), *missum* (two), hissing out the two 's's over and over again, day and night.

So, we always knew that this had to be, and here we are now with only one chapter left. At least it contains some nice stories. Well, I suggest that you now console yourself for having come so near to the end by revising the first nine chapters (what a lovely suggestion!)

Chapter 10

Nunc est legendum

You have now learnt a great deal of Latin and are in a position to sit back and enjoy the fruits of your labours! When the poet Horace felt that he had done a decent day's work and was ready for a quick jar to refresh himself, he used, no doubt, to repeat his old tag *nunc est bibendum* ("now is the time for drinking"). Well in your case, now is the time for reading (*legendum*); here we have some fine Latin passages, all penned specially for your enjoyment. Hooray!

Exercise 10.1

Read the following passage (do not write a translation) and answer the questions below in English. Complete sentences are not required.

Atalanta is warned against marriage

1   *ōlim puellam Atalantam terruit deus, <u>quī</u> dīxit "<u>marītum</u> habēre nōn <u>dēbēs</u>". Atalanta pulchra et clāra erat; et multī virī Atalantam <u>dūcere</u> magnopere cupiēbant. itaque contrā virōs quī Atalantam <u>dūcere</u> cupiēbant, puella currēbat, et*
5   *quod <u>marītum</u> habēre timuit, dīcēbat "marītum habēre <u>nūllum</u> cupiō <u>nisi</u> virum <u>quī</u> mē superat; et hastā necāre cōnstituī virōs <u>quī</u> mē nōn superant." multī virī contrā puellam cucurrērunt; superāvit tamen puellam <u>nēmō</u>.*

quī = who
marītus, -ī, m. = husband
dēbeō, -ēre, -uī, -itum = I ought, must
dūcō: here = marry
nūllus, -a, -um (irreg.) = not any, no
nisi (here) = except
nēmō = no one

(a) In lines 1-2 what did the god tell Atalanta?
(b) In lines 2-3 why did many men want to marry Atalanta?
(c) In lines 3-4 what did she do first with the men who wanted to marry her?
(d) In lines 5-6 what would happen to the man who beat her in the race?
(e) In lines 6-7 what would happen to the men who failed to beat her?
(f) In lines 6-7 how would she carry out this threat?
(g) In lines 7-8, *multī … cucurrērunt;* how does this tell us that Atalanta was an exceptionally attractive girl?
(h) In line 8 what is achieved by the word order of *superāvit … nēmō*?

Exercise 10.2

Translate the following passage into good English:

Hippomenes appears on the scene

1 *multī virī contrā Atalantam cucurrērunt et multōs puella*
  hastā necāvit. sed puer Hippomenēs <u>quī</u> in Atalantae
  patriā erat, virōs vīdit <u>quī</u> contrā Atalantam cucurrērunt, et
  rīsit et dīxit, "<u>stultī</u> fuērunt virī <u>quī</u> contrā puellam
5 *cucurrērunt; multōs iam hastā necāvit; mē tamen nōn*
  necāvit." sed subitō puellam vīdit et statim amāvit et
  <u>dūcere</u> cupiēbat.

quī = who (sing. and pl.)

stultus, -a, -um = stupid

dūcō: here = marry

Exercise 10.3

Study the following passage and answer the questions below in English. Complete sentences are not required.

How Hippomenes won the race; but the end is not too happy

1 *dea <u>Venus</u> puerō tria <u>aurea</u> <u>māla</u> dedit; Hippomenēs*
  fortiter contrā puellam cucurrit, sed puella superābat;
  <u>ter</u> igitur puer <u>mālum</u> ad terram iēcit, et <u>ter</u> puella stetit
  et <u>mālum</u> cēpit; sīc tandem puer puellam superāvit, iam
5 *puella puerum amāvit; laetī erant. sed dea, quod <u>grātī</u>*
  nōn fuērunt, puerum et puellam <u>pūnīvit</u>.

Venus, f. (3rd. dec.) = Venus,
  goddess of love
aureus, -a, -um = golden
mālum, -ī, n. = apple
ter = three times
grātus, -a, -um = grateful
pūnio, -īre, -īvī, -ītum = I punish

(a) In line 1 what case is *puerō* ?
(b) *cucurrit* (line 2): give the person and tense of this word. What is the first person singular of its present tense?
(c) Give two examples from the passage of a preposition followed by a noun: translate the preposition and noun in each case.
(d) In lines 2-4 explain why we have *superābat* in line 2, but *superāvit* in line 4.
(e) *cēpit:* (line 4): from which verb does this come and of which English word does it remind you?
(f) *cēpit* (line 4): what would the 3rd person singular of the imperfect of this verb be?
(g) In line 4 what Latin word is the subject of *superāvit?* And in line 5 what Latin word is the object of *amāvit?*
(h) In lines 5-6 which Latin word is the subject of *pūnīvit?*

Exercise 10.4

Using the vocabulary given below, translate into Latin:

(i)   We are preparing the food.
(ii)   The woman sees the maid-servant.

I prepare = *parō* (1); food = *cibus, cibī*, m.; woman = *fēmina, fēminae*, f.;

maid-servant = *ancilla, -ae*, f.; I see = *videō* (2)

Note how, instead of giving a verb's principal parts, we can write (1) for 1st conjugation and (2) for 2nd conjugation, etc.

Exercise 10.5

Study the following passage (do not write a translation) and answer the questions below in English. Complete sentences are not required.

The god Phoebus Apollo is punished by Jupiter

1	*Iuppiter deōs rēxit; Phoebus Apollō magnus deus erat;*
	ōlim Iuppiter Phoebō magnopere īrātus erat et dīxit deō
	"per ūnum annum in terrā servus esse dēbēs" et
	Phoebum dē caelō ad terram iēcit. ibi incolās rogāvit "ubi
5	*sum?" respondērunt incolae "in Graeciā es, in Thessaliā".*
	rogāvit iterum "quis vōs regit?" respondērunt "nōs regit
	Admētus". dīxit Apollō "dūcite mē ad Admētum."

Iuppiter = Jupiter, King of the gods
Phoebus Apollō = the god of light
    and prophecy
dēbeō, -ēre, -uī, -itum = I ought, must
Graecia, -ae, f. = Greece
Thessalia, -ae, f. = Thessaly, a part
    of Greece

(a) In line 1 what are we told about Jupiter (note how he is spelt in Latin)?
(b) In line 2 *Phoebō* is dative. In Latin *īrātus* is followed by the dative; but how should we translate *Phoebō.........īrātus* into good English?
(c) In line 3 what was Apollo's punishment?
(d) In line 3 how should we translate *esse dēbēs* to give the required sense?
(e) In lines 4-5 what did Apollo do first on coming to earth?
(f) In line 6 what did he do next?
(g) In lines 7-8 and next?
(h) In line 8 in what sort of dwelling do you think Admetus lived?

Exercise 10.6

Translate the following passage into good English:

Alcestis, his wife, agrees to die instead of Admetus

1	*Admētus vir bonus erat; numquam Phoebum miserum*
	fēcit. deus tandem ad caelum discēdēbat et Admētō
	dīxit, "quod bonus dominus erās, ubi ad Tartarum
	discēdere dēbēs, sī alius prō tē discēdere cupit, tū
5	*discēdere nōn dēbēs". Admētus, ubi ad Tartarum*
	discēdere dēbuit, multōs rogāvit. discēdere tamen prō
	Admētō nōn cupīvērunt. sed tandem Alcēstis prō marītō
	discēdere cōnstituit.

Tartarus,- i, m. = the Underworld
sī = if
alius = another (person)
prō + abl. (here) = instead of
dēbeō, -ēre, -ui, -itum = I ought,
    must
marītus, marītī, m. = husband

Exercise 10.7

Study the following passage and answer the questions below. Complete sentences are not required.

A happy ending

1   *Admētum, quod <u>marīta</u> discessit miserum, subitō cum*
amīcīs <u>vīsit</u> Herculēs; cantābant et clāmābant, et
servum rogāvit Herculēs " cūr miserī estis?" respondit
servus "quod Alcēstis <u>mortua</u> est". statim Herculēs <u>ipse</u>
5   *cum <u>Lētō</u> pugnāvit. Herculēs <u>Lētum</u> superat et cum*
fēminā ad Admētum venit. Admētus, ubi fēminam vīdit,
"Alcēstis est" clāmāvit et laetus erat.

marīta, -ae, f. = wife
vīsō, vīsere, vīsī, vīsum = I visit
mortuus, -a, -um = dead
ipse = himself
Lētum, -i, n. = Death

(a) In lines 1-2 *Admētum* is the object of which verb?
(b) In line 1 what agrees with *Admētum?*
(c) In line 2 put *cantābant* and *clāmābant* into the perfect tense.
(d) Give examples of a preposition followed by its case, and translate these examples.
(e) *miserī* (line 3): if all the slaves were women, what would this word be?
(f) *fēminam* (line 6): of what English word does this remind you?
(g) *vīdit* (line 6): from what Latin verb does this come? And what would it become in the present tense?

Exercise 10.8

Using the vocabulary given below, translate into Latin:

(i)   The farmer is building a wall.
(ii) The queen frightens the girl.

farmer = *agricola, -ae*, m.; wall = *mūrus, -ī*, m; I build = *aedificō* (1);
queen = *rēgīna, -ae*, f.; I frighten = *terreō* (2); girl = *puella, -ae*, f.

Exercise 10.9

Study the following passage (do not write a translation) and answer the questions below in English. Complete sentences are not required.

The Athenians have to send some boys and girls to the Minotaur (a famous monster).

1   *Aegeus <u>Athēnās</u> regēbat; filium habuit; filius Thēseus
     erat. <u>Crētam</u> īnsulam regēbat Mīnōs; etiam Mīnōs filium
     habuit <u>Mīnōtaurum, quī</u> <u>et</u> vir <u>et</u> <u>taurus</u> erat. Mīnōs contrā
     Athēnās bellum saevum diū faciēbat; et <u>Athēnārum</u>*
5   *incolae septem puerōs et septem puellās trāns undās ad
     <u>Crētam</u> mittere <u>dēbuērunt</u> ad Mīnōtaurum.*

Athēnae, -ārum, f. pl. = Athens*
Crēta, -ae, f. = Crete
Mīnōtaurus, -ī, m. = the Minotaur
quī = who
et...et = both... and
taurus,-ī, m. = a bull
dēbeō, -ēre, -uī, -itum = I ought, must

__N.B.__ many cities had plural names.

(a) In lines 1-2 who was *Aegeus?* And who was *Mīnōs?*
(b) In lines 1-2 who was *Thēseus?*
(c) In line 2 what sort of place was Crete?
(d) In line 3 how is the son of *Mīnōs* described?
(e) In lines 4-5 what do we learn about the war? (Answer this one in full.)
(f) In lines 5-7 what are we told the Athenians had to do?
(g) In line 6 how did the boys and girls travel to Crete?

Exercise 10.10

Translate the following passage into good English:

Theseus goes with the young Athenians and is given a thread by Ariadne which enables him to trace his way out of the labyrinth.

1   *Thēseus cum puerīs et puellīs ad Crētam nāvigāre
     cōnstituit. Mīnōs filiam habuit; filia erat <u>Ariadna</u>; ubi
     puerī et puellae ad Crētam vēnērunt, vīdit <u>Ariadna</u>
     <u>rēgulum</u> et amāvit; et <u>filum</u> rēgulō dedit. puerōs et*
5   *puellās servī ad Mīnōtaurum, <u>quī</u> labyrinthum habitābat,
     dūxērunt: ibi septem puellae et sex puerī miserī erant et
     perterritī. septimus tamen puer, Thēseus, nōn timuit, sed
     Mīnōtaurum necāvit et auxiliō filī ex <u>labyrinthō</u> discessit.*

Ariadna, -ae, f. = she is usually
   known in English by her
   Greek name Ariadne
rēgulus, -ī, m. here = prince
filum, -ī, n. = a thread
quī = who
labyrinthus, -ī, m. = a labyrinth,
   a large maze-like building

Exercise 10.11

Study the following passage and answer the questions below in English. Complete sentences are not required.

Theseus returns home, but deserts Ariadne, who finds a glorious husband.

1 *Thēseus cum amīcīs suīs et cum Ariadnā ad patriam laetus nāvigābat; sed erat <u>ingrātus</u> et Ariadnam <u>in Naxō</u>, īnsulā, <u>relīquit</u>. ibi deus Bacchus Ariadnam vīdit et amāvit et <u>dūxit</u>. sed Thēseus, ubi in patriam ex magnō*
5 *perīculō tūtus vēnit, statim miser fuit.*

ingrātus –a – um = ungrateful
in Naxō = in Naxos
relinquō, relinquere, relīquī, relictum = I leave (transitive)
dūcō (here) = I marry

(a) In line 2 which words agree with *Thēseus*? Translate them both.
(b) *nāvigābat* (line 2): put this word into the perfect.
(c) *relīquit* (line 3): put this word into the plural.
(d) Mention all the prepositions plus a case in this passage and translate them all with their nouns.
(e) *amāvit* (line 4): what is the object of this word?
(f) *patriam* (line 4): of what English word does this remind you?
(g) *ex magnō perīculō* (lines 4-5): put *magnō perīculō* into the plural.
(h) Put all the adjectives in this passage into their feminine equivalent – keeping the right case and number e.g. for *laetus* put *laeta*.
(i) **(Bonus question)** See if you can find out why Theseus *statim miser fuit*.

Exercise 10.12

Using the vocabulary given below, translate into Latin:

(i)   The queen is holding a book.
(ii)   The horse is watching the poet.

queen = *rēgīna, -ae*, f.;   I hold = *teneō* (2); book = *liber, librī*, m.;   horse = *equus, -ī*, m.;
I watch = *spectō* (1);   poet = *poēta, -ae*, m.

And finally, to round things off, here is your last vocabulary.

Vocabulary 10

cōnsūmō, -ere, cōnsūmpsī, consūmptum =
    I eat, consume
legō, -ere, lēgī, lēctum = I read, choose
locus, -ī, m. = place
lūdō, -ere, lūsī, lūsum = I play
maneō, -ēre, mānsī, mānsum = I remain
moveō, -ēre, mōvī, mōtum = I move
    (transitive)
-ne?: introduces a question
numquam = never
ostendō, -ere, ostendī, ostentum = I show
parō, -āre, -āvī, -ātum = I prepare

pōnō, -ere, posuī, positum = I put, place
prope (+ acc.) = near
respondeō, -ēre, respondī, respōnsum =
    I reply
rīdeō, -ēre, rīsī, rīsum = I laugh
teneō, -ēre, tenuī, tentum = I hold
terra, -ae, f. = land, earth
terreō, -ēre, -uī, -itum = I frighten, terrify
ubi = when
ubi? = where?
via, -ae, f. = road, street, way
videō, -ēre, vīdī, vīsum = I see

All these are already old friends, aren't they? But it's nice to know that you know them, isn't it?

So now, farewell! But fear ye not, we shall soon meet again in Book 2.

Vocabulary: Latin-English

ā, ab (+ abl.) = from, by

absum, abesse, āfuī (goes like *sum*) = I am absent

ad (+ acc.) = to, towards, at

adsum, adesse, adfuī = I am present

aedificō, -āre, -āvī, -ātum = I build

ager, agrī, m. = field

agricola, -ae, m. = farmer

altus, -a, -um = deep, high

ambulō, -āre, -āvī, -ātum = I walk

amīcus, -ī, m. = friend

amō, amāre, amāvī, amātum = I love, like

ancilla, -ae, f. = maid-servant

aqua, -ae, f. = water

audiō, -īre, -īvī, -ītum = I hear, listen to

aurum, -ī, n. = gold

auxilium, -iī, n. = help

bellum, -ī, n. = war

bene = well

bibō, -ere, bibī = I drink

bonus, -a, -um = good

caelum, -ī, n. = sky

cantō, -āre, -āvī, -ātum = I sing

capiō, -ere, cēpī, captum = I take, capture

cibus, -ī, m. = food

clāmō, -āre, -āvī, -ātum = I shout

clārus, -a, -um = famous, clear, bright

cōnstituō, -ere, cōnstituī, cōnstitūtum = I decide

cōnsūmō, -ere, cōnsūmpsī, cōnsūmptum = I eat, consume

contrā (+ acc.) = against

cum (+ abl.) = with, together with

cupiō, -ere, -īvī, -ītum = I want, desire

cūr? = why?

currō, -ere, cucurrī, cursum = I run

dē (+ abl.) = down from, concerning

dea, -ae, f. = goddess (dat. and abl. pl. = *deābus*)

decem = ten

decimus = tenth

deinde = then, next

dēleō, dēlēre, dēlēvī, dēlētum = I destroy

deus, deī, m. (irreg.) = god

dīcō, dīcere, dīxī, dictum = I say

discēdō, -ere, discessī, discessum = I depart

diū (adverb) = for a long time

dīxī: see *dīcō*

dō, dăre, dedī, dătum = I give

dominus, -ī, m. = master, lord

dormiō, -īre, -īvī, -ītum = I sleep

dūcō, -ere, dūxī, ductum = I lead

duo, duae, duo = two

ē (+ abl.) = out of

egŏ = I

equus, equī, m. = horse

et = and

etiam = even, also

faciō, -ere, fēci, factum = I do, make

ex (+ abl.) = out of

fēmina, -ae, f. = woman

fessus, -a, -um = tired

festīnō, -āre, -āvī, -ātum = I hurry

fīlia, -ae, f. = daughter (dat. and abl. pl.: *fīliābus*)

fīlius, fīliī, m. (irreg.) = son

forte = by chance

fortiter = bravely

fuī = see *sum*

gladius, gladiī, m. = sword

habeō, -ēre, -uī, -itum = I have

habitō, -āre, -āvī, -ātum = I inhabit, live, dwell

hasta, -ae, f. = spear

hīc = here

iaciō, -ere, iēcī, iactum = I throw

iam = now, already

ibi = there

igitur = therefore (not generally written 1st word in clause)

in (+ abl.) = in, on

in (+ acc.) = into, on to

incola, -ae, c. = inhabitant

īnsula, -ae, f. = island

intrō, -āre, -āvī, -ātum = I enter, go (+ in + acc.)

īra, -ae, f. = anger

īrātus, -a, -um = angry

Ītalia, -ae, f. = Italy

itaque = therefore, and so

iterum = again

iubeō, -ēre, iussī, iussum = I order

labōrō, -āre, -āvī, -ātum = I work, labour

laetus, -a, -um = happy
laudō, -āre, -āvī, -ātum = I praise
legō, -ere, lēgī, lēctum = I read, choose
liber, librī, m. = book
locus, -ī, m. = place
lūdō, -ere, lūsī, lūsum = I play
magister, magistrī, m. = teacher, master
magnopere = greatly
magnus, -a, -um = big, great
malus, -a, -um = bad
maneō, -ēre, mānsī, mānsum = I remain, stay
mē = me (accusative)
meus, -a, -um = my
miser, -era, -erum = wretched
mittō, -ere, mīsī, missum = I send
moneō, -ēre, -uī, -itum = I warn, advise
moveō, -ēre, mōvī, mōtum = I move (transitive)
mox = soon
multus, -a, -um = much, many
mūrus, -ī, m. = wall
nauta, -ae, m. = sailor
nāvigō, -āre, -āvī, -ātum = I sail
-ne?: introduces a question
necō, necāre, necāvī, necātum = I kill, murder
nōn = not
nōnus = ninth
nōs = we (nom.) or us (acc.)
noster, nostra, nostrum = our
nōtus, -a, -um = well-known
novem = nine
novus, -a, -um = new
numquam = never
nūntius, nūntiī, m. = messenger, message
ō = o!
octāvus, -a, -um = eighth
octō = eight
ōlim = once upon a time
oppidum, -ī, n. = town
oppugnō, -āre, -āvī, -ātum = I attack (a place)
ostendō, -ere, ostendī, ostentum = I show
parō, -āre, -āvī, -ātum = I prepare
parvus, -a, -um = small
patria, -ae, f. = fatherland
pecūnia, -ae, f. = money
per (+ acc.) = through, along
perīculum, -ī, n. = danger
perterritus, -a, -um = terrified
poēta, -ae, m. = poet
pōnō, -ere, posuī, positum = I place, put
portō, -āre, -āvī, -ātum = I carry

prīmus, -a, -um = first
proelium, -iī, n. = battle
prope (+ acc.) = near
puella, -ae, f. = girl
puer, puerī, m. = boy
pugnō, -āre, -āvī, -ātum = I fight
pulcher, pulchra, pulchrum = beautiful
quārtus, -a, -um = fourth
quattuor = four
quid? = what?
quīnque = five
quīntus, -a, -um = fifth
quis? = who?
quod = because
rēgīna, -ae, f. = queen
regō, -ere, rēxī, rēctum = I rule
respondeō, -ēre, respondī, respōnsum = I reply
rīdeō, -ēre, rīsī, rīsum = I laugh, smile
rogō, -āre, -āvī, -ātum = I ask, ask for
Rōmānus, -a, -um = Roman
sacer, sacra, sacrum = sacred
saepe = often
saevus, -a, -um = savage
sagitta, -ae, f. = arrow
scrībō, -ere, scrīpsī, scriptum = I write
scūtum, -ī, n. = shield
secundus, -a, -um = second
sed = but
semper = always
septem = seven
septimus, -a, -um = seventh
servus, -ī, m. = slave
sex = six
sextus, a, um = sixth
sīc = thus
socius, -iī, m. = ally
spectō, -āre, -āvī, -ātum = I watch
statim = immediately
stō, stāre, stetī, stătum = I stand
subitō = suddenly
sum, esse, fuī (irreg.) = I am
superō, -āre, -āvī, -ātum = I overcome
suus, sua, suum = his (own), her (own), its (own)
    or their (own)
tamen = however (not generally written first word
    in clause)
tandem = at last
tē = you (singular, acc.)
templum, -ī, n. = temple
teneō, -ēre, tenuī, tentum = I hold

terra, -ae, f. = land, earth
terreō, -ēre, -uī, -itum = I frighten, terrify
tertius, -a, -um = third
timeō, -ēre, -uī = I fear
trāns (+ acc.) = across
trēs, tria = three
tū = you (singular)
turba, -ae, f. = crowd, disturbance
tūtus, -a, -um = safe
tuus, -a, -um = your (belonging to you (sing.))
ubi = when
ubi? = where?
unda, -ae, f. = wave

ūnus, -a, -um (irreg.) = one
validus, -a, -um = strong
veniō, -īre, vēnī, ventum = I come
ventus, -ī, m. = wind
verbum, -ī, n. = word
vester, vestra, vestrum = your (belonging to you (pl.))
via, -ae, f. = road, street, way
videō, -ēre, vīdī, vīsum = I see
vīnum, -ī, n. = wine
vir, virī, m. (irreg.) = man (as opposed to woman)
vocō, -āre, -āvī, -ātum = I call
vōs = you (plural) (nom. or acc.)

Vocabulary: English-Latin

About (concerning) = *dē* (+ abl.)
Absent, I am = *absum, abesse, āfuī*
Across = *trāns* (+ acc.)
Advise, I = *moneō, -ēre, -uī, -itum*
Again = *iterum*
Against = *contrā* (+ acc.)
Ally = *socius, -iī*, m.
Along = *per* (+ acc.)
Already = *iam*
Also = *etiam*
Always = *semper*
Am, I = *sum, esse, fuī* (irreg.)
And = *et*
Anger = *īra, -ae*, f.
Angry = *īrātus, -a, -um*
Arrow = *sagitta, -ae*, f.
Ask, I = *rogō, -āre, -āvī, -ātum*
Ask for, I = *rogō, -āre, -āvī, -ātum*
At = *ad* (+ acc.)
At last = *tandem*
Attack (a place), I = *oppugnō, -āre, -āvī, -ātum*
Bad = *malus, -a, -um*
Battle = *proelium, -iī*, n.
Beautiful = *pulcher, pulchra, pulchrum*
Because = *quod*
Big = *magnus, -a, -um*
Book = *liber, librī*, m.
Boy = *puer, puerī*, m.
Bravely = *fortiter*
Bright = *clārus, -a, -um*
Build, I = *aedificō, -āre, -āvī, -ātum*
But = *sed*
Capture, I = *capiō, -ere, cēpī, captum*
Carry, I = *portō, -āre, -āvī, -ātum*
Choose, I = *legō, -ere, lēgī, lēctum*
Clear = *clārus, -a, -um*
Come, I = *veniō, -īre, vēnī, ventum*
Concerning = *dē* (+ abl.)
Crowd = *turba, -ae*, f.
Danger = *perīculum, -ī*, n.
Daughter = *fīlia, -ae*, f. (dat. and abl. pl. = *fīliābus*)
Decide, I = *cōnstituō, -ere, cōnstituī, cōnstitūtum*

Deep = *altus, -a, -um*
Depart, I = *discēdō, -ere, discessī, discessum*
Desire, I = *cupiō, -ere, -īvī, -ītum*
Destroy, I = *dēleō, dēlēre, dēlēvī, dēlētum*
Do, I = *faciō, -ere, fēci, factum*
Down from = *dē* (+ abl.)
Drink, I = *bibō, -ere, bibī*
Earth = *terra, -ae*, f.
Eat, I = *cōnsūmō, -ere, cōnsūmpsī, cōnsūmptum*
Eight = *octō*
Eighth = *octāvus, -a, -um*
Enter = *intrō, -āre, -āvī, -ātum*
Even = *etiam*
Famous = *clārus, -a, -um*
Farmer = *agricola, -ae*, m.
Fatherland = *patria, -ae*, f.
Fear, I = *timeō, -ēre, -uī*
Field = *ager, agrī*, m.
Fifth = *quīntus, -a, -um*
Fight, I = *pugnō, -āre, -āvī, -ātum*
First = *prīmus, -a, -um*
Five = *quīnque*
Food = *cibus, -ī*, m.
For a long time = *diū*
Four = *quattuor*
Fourth = *quārtus, -a, -um*
Friend = *amīcus, -ī*, m.
From = *ā, ab* (+ abl.)
Girl = *puella, -ae*, f.
Give, I = *dō, dāre, dedī, dătum*
God = *deus, deī*, m. (irreg.)
Goddess = *dea, -ae*, f. (dat. and abl. pl. = *deābus*)
Gold = *aurum, -ī*, n.
Good = *bonus, -a, -um*
Great = *magnus, -a, -um*
Greatly = *magnopere*
Happy = *laetus, -a, -um*
Have, I = *habeō, -ēre -uī, -itum*
Hear, I = *audiō, -īre, -īvī, -ītum*
Help (noun) = *auxilium, -iī*, n.
Her (own) = *suus, sua, suum*
Here = *hīc*
High = *altus, -a, -um*

His (own) = *suus, sua, suum*
Hold, I = *teneō, -ēre, tenuī, tentum*
Horse = *equus, equī*, m.
Hurry, I = *festīnō, -āre, -āvī, -ātum*
I = *egŏ*
Immediately = *statim*
In = *in* (+ abl.)
Inhabit, I = *habitō, -āre, -āvī, -ātum*
Inhabitant = *incola, -ae*, c.
Into = *in* (+ acc.)
Island = *īnsula, -ae*, f.
Its (own) = *suus, sua, suum*
Kill, I = *necō, necāre, necāvī, necātum*
Land = *terra, -ae*, f.
Large = *magnus, -a, -um*
Laugh, I = *rīdeō, -ēre, rīsī, rīsum*
Lead, I = *dūcō, -ere, dūxī, ductum*
Like, I = *amō, amāre, amāvī, amātum*
Listen to, I = *audiō, -īre, -īvī, -ītum*
Little = *parvus, -a, -um*
Live (inhabit), I = *habitō, -āre, -āvī, -ātum*
Lord = *dominus, -ī*, m.
Love, I = *amō, amāre, amāvī, amātum*
Maid-servant = *ancilla, -ae*, f.
Make, I = *faciō, -ere, fēcī, factum*
Man (as opposed to woman) = *vir, virī*, m. (irreg.)
Many; *see* much
Master = *dominus, -ī*, m.; *magister, magistrī*, m
Message = *nūntius, nūntiī*, m.
Messenger = *nūntius, nūntiī*, m.
Money = *pecūnia, -ae*, f.
Move, I (transitive) = *moveō, -ēre, mōvī, mōtum*
Much (plural = many) = *multus, -a, -um*
Murder, I = *necō, -āre, āvī, ātum*
My = *meus, -a, -um*
Near = *prope* (+ acc.)
Never = *numquam*
New = *novus, -a, -um*
Next = *deinde*
Nine = *novem*
Ninth = *nōnus*
Not = *nōn*
Now = *iam*
O! = *ō*
Often = *saepe*
On = *in* (+ abl.)
On to = *in* (+ acc.)
Once upon a time = *ōlim*
One = *ūnus, -a, -um* (irreg.)
Order, I = *iubeō, -ēre, iussī, iussum*

Our = *noster, nostra, nostrum*
Out of = *ex, ē* (+ abl.)
Overcome, I = *superō, -āre, -āvī, -ātum*
Place (noun) = *locus, -ī*, m.
Place, I = *pōnō, -ere, posuī, positum*
Play, I = *lūdō, -ere, lūsī, lūsum*
Poet = *poēta, -ae*, m.
Praise, I = *laudō, -āre, -āvī, -ātum*
Prepare, I = *parō, -āre, -āvī, -ātum*
Present, I am = *adsum, adesse, adfuī*
Pretty = *pulcher, pulchra, pulchrum*
Put, I = *pōnō, -ere, posuī, positum*
Queen = *rēgīna, -ae*, f.
Read, I = *legō, -ere, lēgī, lēctum*
Remain, I = *maneō, -ēre, mānsī, mānsum*
Reply, I = *respondeō, -ēre, respondī, respōnsum*
Road = *via, -ae*, f.
Roman (adjective) = *Rōmānus, -a, -um*
Rule, I = *regō, -ere, rēxī, rēctum*
Run, I = *currō, -ere, cucurrī, cursum*
Sacred = *sacer, sacra, sacrum*
Safe = *tūtus, -a, -um*
Sail, I = *nāvigō, -āre, -āvī, -ātum*
Sailor = *nauta, -ae*, m.
Savage = *saevus, -a, -um*
Say, I = *dīcō, dīcere, dīxī, dictum*
Second = *secundus, -a, -um*
See, I = *videō, -ēre, vīdī, vīsum*
Send, I = *mittō, -ere, mīsī, missum*
Seven = *septem*
Seventh = *septimus, -a, -um*
Shield = *scūtum, -ī*, n.
Shout, I = *clāmō, -āre, -āvī, -ātum*
Show, I = *ostendō, -ere, ostendī, ostentum*
Sing, I = *cantō, -āre, -āvī, -ātum*
Six = *sex*
Sixth = *sextus, -a, -um*
Sky = *caelum, -ī*, n.
Slave = *servus, -ī*, m.
Slave-girl = *ancilla, -ae*, f.
Sleep, I = *dormiō, -īre, -īvī, ītum*
Small = *parvus, -a, -um*
Smile, I = *rīdeō, -ēre, rīsī, rīsum*
Son = *fīlius, fīliī* m. (irreg.)
Soon = *mox*
Spear = *hasta, -ae*, f.
Stand, I = *stō, stāre, stetī, stătum*
Street = *via, -ae*, f.
Strong = *validus, -a, -um*
Suddenly = *subitō*

Sword = *gladius, gladiī*, m.
Take (seize), I = *capiō, -ere, cēpī, captum*
Teacher = *magister, magistrī,* m.
Temple = *templum, -ī*, n.
Ten = *decem*
Tenth = *decimus*
Terrified = *perterritus, -a, -um*
Terrify, I = *terreō, -ēre, -uī, -itum*
Their (own) = *suus, sua, suum*
Then = *deinde*
There = *ibi*
Therefore = *igitur* (not generally written first word in clause); *itaque*
Third = *tertius, -a, -um*
Three = *trēs, tria*
Through = *per* (+ acc.)
Throw, I = *iaciō, -ere, iēcī, iactum*
Thus = *sīc*
Tired = *fessus, -a, -um*
To, towards = *ad* (+ acc.)
Together with = *cum* (+ abl.)
Towards = *ad* (+ acc.)
Town = *oppidum, -ī,* n.
Two = *duŏ, duae, duŏ*
Walk, I = *ambulō, -āre, -āvī, -ātum*
Wall = *mūrus, -ī,* m.
Want, I = *cupiō, -ere, -īvī, -ītum*
War = *bellum, -ī,* n.

Warn, I = *moneō, -ēre, -uī, -itum*
Watch, I = *spectō, -āre, -āvī, -ātum*
Water = *aqua, -ae,* f.
Wave = *unda, -ae,* f.
Way (i.e. road) = *via, -ae,* f.
We = *nōs*
Weary = *fessus, -a, -um*
Well = *bene*
Well-known = *nōtus, -a, -um*
What? = *quid?*
When (conjunction) = *ubi*
Where? = *ubi?*
Who? = *quis?*
Why? = *cūr?*
Wicked = *malus, -a, -um*
Wind = *ventus, -ī,* m.
Wine = *vīnum, -ī,* n.
With = *cum* (+ abl.)
Woman = *fēmina, -ae,* f.
Word = *verbum, -ī,* n.
Work, I = *labōrō, -āre, -āvī, -ātum*
Wretched = *miser, -era, -erum*
Write, I = *scrībō, -ere, scrīpsī, scrīptum*
You (singular) = *tū*
You (plural) = *vōs*
Your (belonging to you (singular)) = *tuus, -a, -um*
Your (belonging to you (plural)) = *vester, vestra, vestrum*